P9-CMC-784

ON THE PASSION OF CHRIST
ACCORDING TO THE
FOUR EVANGELISTS

THOMAS À KEMPIS

ON THE PASSION
OF CHRIST
ACCORDING TO
THE
FOUR EVANGELISTS

Prayers and Meditations

Translated by
Joseph N. Tylenda, S.J.

IGNATIUS PRESS   SAN FRANCISCO

Cover art: *Crucifixion* (detail)
Matthias Grünewald
A panel from the Isenheim Altar
Musée d'Unterlinden, Colmar
Erich Lessing/Art Resource, New York

Cover design by Roxanne Mei Lum

ISBN 978-0-89870-993-3
Library of Congress Control Number 2003115825
Printed in the United States of America ∞

CONTENTS

INTRODUCTION

Thomas à Kempis was born in Kempen, Germany, some forty miles north of Cologne, toward the end of 1379 or the beginning of 1380. His family name was Hemerken; his father, John, was a blacksmith and his mother, Gertrude, was a schoolmistress. Thomas' early education was had in his native town, but in 1392, at age thirteen, when it was time to go elsewhere to further his studies, he was sent to Deventer in the Low Countries, where Jan, his older brother by some fifteen years, had studied. At the time of Thomas' arrival there, his brother, who in 1390 had earlier entered the Brethren of the Common Life, was then a canon at their monastery in Windesheim. Hence, Thomas first visited his brother and informed him of his plans to study at Jan's alma mater. Since the school in Deventer was operated by the Brethren, Thomas, on leaving Windesheim, carried with him Jan's letter recommending him to Florens Radewijns (ca. 1350–1400), Master of the Deventer school.

Radewijns was one of the early followers of Geert Groote (1340–1384), founder of the Brethren and of the popular religious movement known as *Devotio Moderna* (New Devotion). When the piety and spiritual life of the Catholics in the Low Countries began to wane and the people became somewhat slovenly in the practice of their faith, Groote's movement succeeded in renewing devotion in the hearts of his people. Though the movement became known as *Devotio Moderna*, there was actually nothing modern, new, or novel about it, rather it was basically a program of renewal or revitalization of the faith. When Groote died in 1384, Radewijns succeeded him as head of the movement and as superior of the Brethren in Deventer. It was under the latter's supervision that Thomas was educated.

Thomas' course of studies at Deventer lasted seven years, from 1392 to 1399, and upon completing his program of instruction, Radewijns suggested that Thomas visit his brother Jan, who in 1398 had been elected the first prior of the newly founded monastery of Canons Regular of Saint Augustine at Mount Saint Agnes, near Zwolle. Since Thomas had associated with the Brethren in Deventer, he was familiar with their manner of life and their spirituality, so it is not at all strange that he should have requested to become a member of his brother's religious community. In 1399, Jan gladly accepted Thomas as a candidate. Following monastic custom, he was now known as Thomas of Kempen or, as the Latin would have it, *Thomas à Kempis*. He spent the next seven years, from 1399 to 1406, participating in the community's life, sharing their hours of work and prayer, and perfecting his calligraphy, thus developing his ability to copy liturgical and devotional books.

On the feast of Corpus Christi in 1406, which fell on June 10 of that year, Thomas was formally accepted as a member of the Congregation of the Canons Regular of Saint Augustine and was clothed with the congregation's distinctive white habit. In 1408, he pronounced his religious vows and subsequently was ordained a priest in 1414—he was then thirty-four years of age. Thomas twice served as subprior of the community; he was first elected to that office in 1425 and again in 1448. As subprior, he was not only the prior's assistant, but he also fulfilled the important office of Master of Novices. It is quite probable that the four treatises that form his celebrated *The Imitation of Christ* were written during his first term as subprior.

Thomas spent his entire religious life at Mount Saint Agnes, except for a three-year period, 1429 to 1432, when the community went into exile to neighboring Friesland. The see of Utrecht had become vacant in 1423 and a dispute arose as to who was to become the new bishop. When Pope Martin V's appointee was not accepted by the people, the pope placed the diocese under an interdict in 1428. As a result all public celebrations of Mass and the dispensing of the sacraments were forbidden. Because the canons at Mount Saint Agnes chose to be loyal to the pope and to observe the interdict, they refused to yield to the capricious demands of the local citizenry for the sacraments. Hence the monks, in their search for peace and quiet, voluntarily went into exile. This they did in June 1429.

The monks returned to their monastery in 1432, but Thomas was not to return until sometime later. Since his brother Jan, then superior of the House of Bethany in Arnhem, had fallen seriously ill, Thomas left Friesland in September 1431 to assist him in his illness. There he remained until his brother's death on November 4, 1432. Upon Thomas' return to Mount Saint Agnes, he served as community procurator, but in 1448 he was again elected subprior.

From 1425 to 1439, during his years at Mount Saint Agnes, Thomas made a copy of the entire Bible in five volumes, which is now preserved in the Darmstadt Library. In addition to his beloved *The Imitation of Christ*, he produced some three dozen devotional works. The favorites are: *Prayers and Meditations on the Life of Christ*, the second part of which is here presented to the reader, *The Soul's Soliloquy*, *On the Three Tabernacles*, *The Little Garden of Roses*, *The Valley of Lilies*, *On Solitude and Silence*, and *Sermons to Novices*. He likewise wrote biographies of the founders of the *Devotio Moderna*: Geert Groote and Florens Radewijns. At the time of his death Thomas was near completing his *Chronicles of the Canons Regular of Mount St. Agnes.* The date of his death is usually given as July 25, 1471. He was then ninety-two years of age, had spent sixty-five years in religion, and was a priest for fifty-eight years. He was buried in the monastery's east cloister. His remains were removed in 1672 to the church of Saint Joseph in Zwolle, then transferred in 1892 to that of Saint Michael, but when the latter was replaced by a newer church of the same name, the remains were taken there in 1965.

On the Passion of Christ according to the Four Evangelists

At the very beginning of his *The Imitation of Christ*, Thomas reminds the reader that in order to become a follower of Christ one must imitate his life, and to accomplish this he adds: "Let it then be our main concern to meditate on the life of Jesus Christ." [1] It is impossible to imitate Christ without first knowing him, and the best way of getting to know him is by meditating on his life as it is described in the four Gospels. Thomas firmly believed that whoever "meditates devoutly on the most holy life and Passion of our Lord will find all that he needs to make his life worthwhile. In fact, he has no need to go beyond Jesus, for he will discover nothing better. If Jesus Crucified would come into our hearts, how quickly and perfectly we would be instructed in the spiritual life." [2]

Thomas is here undoubtedly speaking from his own experience in using the Gospels as subject matter for his prayer and meditation. When he penned the above citations, he had already spent some twelve years as a religious, [3] and dur-

---

[1] *The Imitation of Christ*, trans. Joseph N. Tylenda, S.J., Vintage Spiritual Classics (New York: Random House, 1998), chap. 1, p. 3.

[2] Ibid., chap. 25, p. 41.

[3] The *Imitation* was most probably written between the years 1425 and 1427.

ing those years much of his prayer was on the Gospel accounts of our Lord's life. It was several years after Thomas
had completed the *Imitation* that he wrote his *Prayers and Meditations on the Life of Christ*. The date of its composition is
uncertain, however. It was most probably written during the
years when he was the community's subprior and Master of
Novices. The purpose Thomas had in composing this work
was similar to that of the *Imitation*, namely, the spiritual benefit of his fellow monks at Mount Saint Agnes.

Prayers and Meditations is divided into four parts. The first deals
with the period from our Lord's Incarnation to the Last Supper and is entitled, "Devout Meditations on the Life and Benefits of Jesus Christ the Savior, together with Thanksgiving";
the second is "On the Passion of Christ according to the Four
Evangelists"; the next is "On the Resurrection of Christ and
His Appearances"; and finally "On the Ascension, Pentecost
and Other Matters". Only the second part of this work, namely
those chapters dealing with Christ's Passion, is here translated, not only because this part attracted the translator more
than the others, but also because this may well have been the
author's favorite part. That Thomas had great devotion to
Christ's Passion is clearly stated in the obituary written by a con-
temporary and appended to Thomas' final work dealing with
the history of their monastery. This unknown author wrote:
"The thought of the Lord's passion filled his heart with love." [4]

Up to the present, only four English translations of the
Prayers and Meditations on the Life of Christ have been pub-
lished. The first appeared in Paris in 1664.[5] The volume gave

[4] *The Chronicles of the Canons Regular of Mount St. Agnes*, trans. J. P. Arthur
(London: Kegan Paul, Trench, Trubner, 1906), p. 144.

[5] *Meditations and Prayers on the Life, Passion, Resurrection, and Ascension of Our
Saviour Jesus Christ* (Paris, 1664). This volume is extremely rare since only a
small number of copies were printed for the exclusive use of the nuns in that
particular monastery.

Thomas Carre as the translator, his true name however was Miles Pinkney (1599–1674), a Catholic priest, who, for some forty years, had been chaplain to the exiled English Canonesses Regular of Saint Augustine in Paris. Carre had previously translated Thomas' *Imitation* in 1636, as well his *Sermons of the Incarnation and Passion* and *Soliloquies* in 1653.[6]

The second translation is that of Henry Lee (fl. 1751–1767?).[7] The volume appeared in 1760, with a second edition in 1762, and Lee readily admits in his preface that he has taken liberties in translating the work. For example, he omitted sections and chapters that he thought offensive to his fellow Protestant coreligionists (i.e., those dealing with the invocation of the saints and with Mary) and enlarges on others emphasizing the Protestant interpretation of the Scriptures. So greatly did he change Thomas' text that a later translator remarks: "The outcome of Mr. Lee's system of 'translation' is that only about three-tenths of his book come from Thomas à Kempis, the rest being Mr. Lee's."[8]

The third translation is that of the Archdeacon Wright and Samuel Kettlewell (1822–1893), which appeared in 1892 with a second edition in 1894. They undertook the project of retranslating Thomas' work because of their dissatisfaction with the Lee translation. In his preface Kettlewell notes: "... [I]n this case, so much of the translator's reflections and references to Scripture are added, that it is difficult to tell what really is Lee's and what belongs to Thomas à

---

[6] See Joseph Gillow, *Bibliographical Dictionary of the English Catholics from the Breach with Rome, in 1534, to the Present Time*, 5 vols. (London: Burns and Oates, 1885–1902), 5:313–17.

[7] *Meditations, with Prayers, on the Life and Loving-kindnesses of Our Lord and Saviour, Jesus Christ* (London: E. Dilly, 1760).

[8] *Prayers and Meditations on the Life of Christ*, trans. W. Duthoit (London: Kegan Paul, Trench, Trubner, 1908), p. xxv.

Kempis." [9] These translators likewise omit passages where Thomas refers to the invocation of the saints, as well as our chapters 26 and 34. Their explanation for these omissions is: "Any words sanctioning some corruption or error prevalent in the Pre-Reformation Church, are carefully excluded." [10]

The next translation is that of William Duthoit (1835–?),[11] which appeared in 1908. This version is definitely faithful to Thomas' work, but is now almost one hundred years old and somewhat Victorian in style. Where Thomas expresses his thought in very concise and succinct Latin, Duthoit often prefers to express the same in an extended paraphrase, undoubtedly to make it easier for the reader to understand.

The translation that we now present to the reader is "On the Passion of Christ according to the Four Evangelists", the second part of Thomas à Kempis' work entitled *Prayers and Meditations on the Life of Christ*. Though it is only a part of the whole, nevertheless, it is more than half of the volume. The translation was made from the critical edition of Thomas' works by Michael Joseph Pohl (1835–1922).[12] At the same time, the translator had the Wright/Kettlewell and Duthoit translations on his desk. He has attempted to keep to Thomas' concise and compact style, as well as to preserve the author's penchant for parallel phrasing.

Thomas takes it for granted that the reader has some familiarity with the Passion accounts as found in the four Gospels, that is, Matthew 26:1—27:65, Mark 14:32—15:47, Luke

[9] *Meditations on the Life of Christ*, trans. Archdeacon Wright and S. Kettlewell (Oxford and London: Parker, 1892), p. xliii.

[10] Ibid. pp. xlvii–xlviii.

[11] See note 8, above.

[12] "De passione Christi secundum scripta quatuor evangelistarum," *Orationes et meditationes de vita Christi*, in *Thomae Hemerken a Kempis opera omnia*, 7 vols. (Freiburg, 1902–1922), 5:55–214.

22:1—23:56, and John 18:1—19:42.[13] He reviews various episodes of Christ's Passion in thirty-five meditations and begins each with a colloquy to Christ, followed by a reflection. It is in these reflections that one encounters echoes of the *Imitation*.

Like all other meditation books, this one is not to be read at one sitting, rather it is to be prayed chapter by chapter. It would be most helpful for the reader first to read a portion of Thomas' text, visualize the scene under consideration, and then quietly and unhurriedly reflect on the same. Make Thomas' prayer your own. Join with him when he addresses the Lord and listen to him when he speaks to you, the reader.

Though these meditations were primarily written for his fellow monks and have references to monastic customs, these latter should prove no obstacle to the attentive reader, for such matters will become clear from the context or are explained in the footnotes.

Finally, the prayer of the translator is that these meditations on the Lord's Passion fill the reader's heart with greater love for Christ, in the same way as the love of Christ's Passion once filled that of the author.

Feast of the Exaltation of the Holy Cross

[13] In writing about Christ's Passion, Thomas is a product of his time, and when he speaks of the role played by the Jews and Romans he reflects the thinking of that age. We ask the reader to keep in mind that he holds a medieval text in hand, and that the Catholic Church, being most sensitive in these matters, would not speak today as Thomas sometimes does.

Chapter I

On the sale of Jesus by the traitor Judas

LORD JESUS CHRIST, Supreme Goodness and Eternal Majesty, I bless and thank you for being unjustly sold by your own disciple for so ignoble and meager a price as thirty pieces of silver.

I praise and glorify you for your patient sufferance of that disloyal disciple, for though you foresaw that he was hastening to betray you, nevertheless, you did not manifest any anger toward him, nor did you speak any harsh words to him. You did not make his evil intentions known to others, nor after so villainous a deed did you remove him from his office or refuse him Holy Communion.

How great is your patience, most gentle Jesus, and how great my impatience!

Alas! How poorly I tolerate a brother when he has said or done something against me. But you, for so long a time and without complaint, have endured your disciple Judas, who would soon sell and betray you, while I, for a paltry insult, quickly yield to anger and think of various ways of vindicating myself or of offering excuses. Where then is my patience, where is my meekness?

 Help me, good Jesus, and instill the virtue of your meekness in my heart in greater abundance, for without your inspiration and special grace I cannot enjoy peace of soul amid this life's many vexations.

*Jesus prays on the Mount of Olives while the disciples sleep (top),
Judas' kiss of betrayal (bottom).*

Chapter 2

On the sorrow and fear that
Jesus experienced

LORD JESUS CHRIST, Creator and Redeemer of all the faithful, I bless and thank you for the sorrowful beginning of your most bitter Passion, for your extreme sadness of soul, and for the anguish and dread you felt in your weak human nature, which you willingly assumed for our sake. When the hour of your betrayal was at hand you were filled with sad-ness and fear.

You were not ashamed to express that sadness openly in the presence of the apostles, saying: *My soul is sorrowful unto death.*[1] O wondrous dispensation of God! Lord of power, who shortly before had fortified your disciples for the com-bat, now you appear as one enfeebled, totally devoid of strength and courage.

You generously uttered that statement in order to comfort us, who are weak and cowardly, lest one of us, being severely tempted, despair of forgiveness and salvation. For if some-one were to feel less than cheerful in bearing his suffering or in experiencing certain weaknesses of his flesh, then he can repeat in his fear and sadness what we read that you yourself had said: *Nevertheless, not as I will but as you will.*[2]

---

[1] Mark 14:34.
[2] Luke 22:42.

19

I ask you, most loving Jesus, my only hope in every difficulty and trial, to permit me to enter with a compassionate heart into the sorrowful beginnings of your most blessed Passion, and from there to rise little by little to the contemplation of its more bitter elements, so that in following you in every step of your sorrows I may find a healing remedy for my soul.

Grant me, for the glory of your name, the patience to suffer whatever trials may come my way, and that, when faced with many afflictions, I may never yield to despair but wholly resign myself to the good pleasure of your eternal will.

Chapter 3

On our Lord's triple prayer, his prostration before the Father and his resignation of will

LORD JESUS CHRIST, Sustainer of angels and Refuge of the desolate, I bless and thank you for your anguished prayer and humble prostrations. On bended knees you thrice prayed, earnestly and devoutly, to your heavenly Father that, if it be possible, the chalice of your Passion be taken from you, however, always adding: *Nevertheless, not as I will, but as you will.*[1]

I praise and glorify you for your strenuous combat against the horror of death and the most bitter sorrows of your Passion. But when the divine love that burned so ardently within you prevailed, it wiped out all human fear.

I praise and thank you for the abundant flow of your bloody sweat, when in your agony you prayed the more fervently—drops of which, contrary to nature, poured profusely from your body.

I adore and glorify you, Creator and Ruler of the heavenly spirits, for your humble acceptance of the angelic comfort, which you did not disdain to receive from the ministering angel. In this way you teach us that, in our weakness, we

[1] Luke 22:42.

Christ in the Garden of Olives

should not seek comfort in transitory things but strive for that which is heavenly.

Good Jesus, with how great an ardent love did you love me! Your prayer was so fervent in my behalf that together with your desire to suffer for me, your warm blood, instead of natural sweat, flowed down upon the ground.

I praise and reverence you with endless honor, Creator of my soul and Exemplar of my life, for your complete resignation, the total abnegation of your will, and your body's natural instincts that made you abhor pain and death. When the hour of your suffering arrived, you spontaneously and willingly resigned yourself to your Father, saying: *Father, not my will, but yours be done.*[2]

By these very words you offered greater glory to your Father and you merited abundantly for us. You thoroughly conquered the devil and clearly demonstrated to all of us faithful that you are our model of perfection, the sign of our salvation, and our way to perfect virtue.

Jesus, may I ever remember and adore you. With great affection of heart, I ask you to grant that I may gain the fruit of your thrice-repeated prayer and with a generous heart to imitate, in the religious state that I have chosen, your example of self-abnegation.

Also grant me the grace courageously to overcome my defiant flesh for the benefit of my soul, to cast out all carnal fear, to pray more frequently and attentively, to enjoy your assistance, to leave every outcome in your hands, to renounce my will thoroughly, and to be ready to suffer whatever comes.

---

[2] Mark 14:36.

Chapter 4

On how the Lord Jesus went to meet his betrayer

LORD JESUS CHRIST, Savior and Deliverer, I bless and thank you for your readiness and willingness to undergo your Passion. After you had offered your thrice-repeated petition to God, your cruel enemies arrived amid the night's darkness, with your betrayer the evil Judas—a large crowd with staves and swords, arms and torches, as if to apprehend a thief. At that moment you went out to meet them saying: *Whom do you seek?* . . . *I am he. If you seek me, let these others go.* [1]

At your first word, so filled with power, their proud defiance was discomfitted and brought to utter confusion, and immediately they all fell backward, collapsing to the ground. What would have happened if you had summoned twelve legions of angels? Since you had come among us to suffer, you chose not to use your divine power but to make known your benign patience. By a single word you showed what power is actually yours, and for a time you permitted the impious to have the upper hand in grievously insulting you. Thus you made it clear that you were willingly entering upon your Passion to bring about our redemption and, thereby, to fulfill the writings of the prophets.

[1] John 18:7–8.

I praise and glorify you, Jesus Christ, most innocent Lamb
of God, for your unspeakable meekness and overwhelming
kindness in not being aroused with wrath against your most
deceitful betrayer or angrily turning away from him. Rather
you kindly deigned to engage him in friendly conversation
calling him, in your usual gentle manner, *Friend*, and you
gave him, though unworthy, a tender kiss with your lips and
lovingly said: *Friend, why have you come?*[2]

With such words as these, you admonished his rashness,
his iniquity, and his disloyalty: *Judas, do you betray the Son of
Man with a kiss?*[3] Even more sadly, he, who once was numbered among the apostles—neither fearing the divine justice
nor swayed by your friendship—did not refrain from extend-
ing his hands to the most heinous of crimes, and now, as
head of this band of ruffians, he gave them as the signal:
Whomever I shall kiss, it is he. Take hold of him.[4] O most wicked
disciple and most loving Master! O base servant and most
faithful Lord!

How admirable your behavior, how wonderful your patience, most gentle and kind Jesus! In the very act of his carrying out this shameful betrayal, you did not forget your old
friendship and affection, but in return for so great an injury done
to you, you exercised your healing power, for when a disciple
cut off the ear of one of the high priest's servants, you restored
it by the touch of your sacred hand. You restrained Peter, then
defending you from those attacking you, saying: *Put back your
sword where it belongs. Am I not to drink the cup which the Father
has given me to drink? Thus it is to be.*[5]

I now ask you, my God, grant me, since I am but a frail
reed, greater patience amid my trials, and may sudden anger

[2] Matthew 26:50.
[3] Luke 22:48.
[4] Mark 14:44.
[5] John 18:11.

never overwhelm me, nor the spirit of revenge inflame me, when my enemies utter insults against me, or when accusations are made of which I know I am innocent. Grant me not to fear my accuser but to receive his allegations in good spirit and to look upon him, who so discourteously blames and slanders me, as a friend.

Let no indignation arise in me for any harshness shown me, nor let any remembrance of unjust offenses remain in me. May your most benign bearing of such evil treatment strengthen my will by granting it patience, as well as the desire to endure even greater trials for love of you.

Chapter 5

On the shameful arrest and leading away of the Lord Jesus

LORD JESUS CHRIST, Hope of the saints and Tower of strength in every tribulation, I bless and thank you for undergoing so violent an arrest by hateful enemies, for the arrogant laying of sacrilegious hands on you by those sent to arrest you, and for the brutal looks and menacing shouts of those carrying arms against you. I bless and thank you for your harsh and cruel binding, for your rough and ruthless detention, for your painful pummeling, and for your being so abruptly dragged away. Amid all this tumult, while you were being rushed to your death by mean-spirited and worthless villains, your dear disciples, who had deserted you, looked upon you from a distance with great sorrow.

Lord, King of kings, you, who have dominion over all creatures and who alone among mortals are truly free, why did you allow yourself to be so violently taken captive and to be so wickedly led away by despicable men, whom you yourself had created and for whom you have always done good?

How grave a crime was committed against you, who are free of all sin, and how rash the insult to your almighty power, when you, Deliverer of souls, were bound with a criminal's cords and were led away captive, as if you were the worst of thieves.

Loving Jesus, supreme Exemplar of virtue, you chose most patiently to suffer this cruelty for us, in order to give us an example of your singular meekness and to fulfill Isaiah's clear prophecy: *He shall be led as a sheep to the slaughter, and shall be dumb as a lamb before his shearer, and he shall not open his mouth. He was offered because it was his own will.*[1]

My soul, show compassion on the sorrow and arrest of the beloved Lord, your God, who voluntarily suffers all this for your sins. May your lament be endless, and may your eyes yield its tears because it is the only Son of God who is being so unworthily treated for you. See, what those impudent men are doing. They hold Jesus captive and take him bound before the high priests Annas and Caiaphas. When arrested, he does not resist; when bound, he does not complain; when led away, he does not protest; when dragged off, he does not rebuke, rather he meekly goes, silent as a lamb and, though innocent, he follows after them and humbly endures it all.

My God, I ask, that the bitter pain you experienced in your sorrowful captivity may often enter into my heart's depths but especially during the night hour of Matins.[2] May it arouse in me a fervent love for this holy prayer, may it banish sloth and make me watchful and eager to persevere in praising you. In this way, and in some measure at least, I may repay you for your love and for all that you have done for me. You were born into this world during the night, and during the night you were betrayed, arrested, and bound with ropes. Therefore, Lord, during night prayer I will be especially mindful of your name and reflect on how greatly you have suffered for me, who am the worst of sinners.

[1] See Isaiah 53:7.
[2] In monastic communities, Matins (now the Office of Readings) was the first and longest of the canonical hours. Now it may be anticipated, but in the author's time it began sometime after midnight and before daybreak.

Chapter 6

On the desertion of our Lord
and the flight of the apostles

LORD JESUS CHRIST, Good Shepherd and gentle Master, I bless and thank you for your utter desertion and abandonment, when, at the moment of your greatest need, all your disciples and acquaintances forsook you and left you alone among your cruel enemies. Your chosen brethren and friends had promised to give their lives and to die for you, but when the time came to prove themselves, they chose flight and deserted you.

I praise and honor you for the sorrow in your heart, by which you painfully endured the cowardice and the flight of your disciples. They abandoned you, their shepherd, in the midst of wolves. They dispersed like a flock of sheep, each going his own way, as you had foretold.

What great sadness, sorrow, and grief filled the hearts of the disciples, when they saw their Lord and Master, for whom they had left all to follow, so violently taken from them and dragged to death.

But you, Lord, who know all things and allow nothing to happen without a good cause, permitted so great a failure in your chosen friends so that a greater good would be theirs in the future. As a result of this lapse, they came face to face with their own frailty and learned to be more compassionate toward their weak brethren, and they themselves, ever afterward, exercised greater caution, were more fervent in spirit, as well as humble and devout.

How useful it would be for me to reflect on this scene at greater length and not to presume that anything great can come from me. Though the grace of new fervor sometimes fills me during prayer, I know not how long it will last, nor what will happen to me in time of temptation. If the very pillars of heaven, the apostles of Christ, quaked in the hour of trial, how then will a frail weakling react when even a slight temptation comes his way?

There are those, Lord, who use harsh terms in admonishing the holy apostles for having so shamefully deserted you. The apostles fled because they had been overwhelmed by fear. But these faultfinders do not see how every day they themselves quickly turn away from the truth—it all depends on how love or hate moves them.

I beg you, dear Lord, to keep me from falling into such madness of heart that I should depart from the holy purpose I have set for myself, but that I should follow you wherever you go, whether it be to life or death. May I never desert you in time of adversity nor yield to the concupiscence of the flesh and consent to sin, but, in my pursuit of virtue and for the love of you, may I prove myself by manfully facing a variety of trials. If I were to give in to my slothfulness, I should lose you, my Supreme Good.

Let not the foot of the proud overtake me because of some good work I have done. Let me not speak presumptuously as did Peter, preferring myself over another or considering myself everyone's equal, rather, by humbly acknowledging my own weakness, may I always act with fear of you.

May Saint Peter's fall and the apostles' flight serve me as a warning against sin rather than be obstacles in my path. Let their return to repentance instill in me the great hope that I too may seek mercy after my own failings; for there is no one so holy that does not sometimes fall into venial sin. If it should happen that I am deserted by friends and acquaintances or am looked upon, by those whom I love, as a stranger and as one who is worthless, then grant me, as a special remedy, to recall your complete desertion and abandonment, that I may readily forego all human consolation, and in some small measure be conformed to you as you undergo your trials.

Gentle Jesus, forgive me for having so often offended you, for so easily turning to vanities, and for not setting my heart on that which I have proposed to do. How often I look back on the amount of time I spent on so many things, all far from important, while I paid no attention to your Passion. You have preceded me along the narrow road, and with eyes dry I pass by as if your sorrows have no effect on me. Remember my foolish heart and instill in it a loving remembrance of your most bitter Passion.

Chapter 7

On Jesus before Annas the high priest

LORD JESUS CHRIST, Guide of our life and Author of our salvation, I bless and thank you for your first arraignment before the high priest Annas, where, after you had been interrogated about various things, you were harshly struck on the cheek for your humble and truthful response.

I praise and glorify you, Christ, glorious King, for enduring the insulting and disgraceful affront by the hand of a shameless servant; when the response left your lips, he directed a heavy blow to your face, saying: *Do you thus answer the high priest?*[1]

Kind Jesus, ever calm in spirit and speech, you did not hesitate to answer him with gentle words: *If I have spoken evil, give testimony of that evil, but if well, why then do you strike me?*[2] O vile and wicked servant, did you not fear to strike the lovable face of your Creator with such hateful hands?

My revered Jesus, how wonderfully you manifested your inexpressible meekness on this occasion, rather than immediately avenging so heinous an insult, you deliberately and calmly corrected the one who struck you.

You, who are one of Christ's followers, reflect and ask yourself whether for the love of God you are able to endure such

[1] John 18:22.
[2] John 18:23.

a slap on the cheek? You, who are unable to endure harsh criticism without yielding to anger, how can you bear such a blow in the face?

You are saddened because of the unjust treatment shown your Lord, but yours is still greater sadness because you feel yourself incapable of bearing even small injuries for the honor of Christ.

You set great goals for yourself and let your thoughts float on high; but at the first words of reproach that you hear, you become terribly disturbed and discover that you are weaker than you first thought. Therefore, go to Jesus and plead more earnestly with him for the virtue of patience.

Good Jesus, strength and power of a soul suffering tribulation, teach me to accept all criticism and reproof with a calm spirit, and let me never show resentment in defending myself because of complaints unjustly made against me. Rather, let me respond to them with gentle silence and, if I must speak, then let me answer my accusers in a pleasant and friendly tone. When I am in the presence of my enemies, put the apt and right words on my lips, and when the hand of the wicked is raised against me, kind Jesus, let a humble, calm, and constant mind be my invulnerable shield.

Chapter 8

On Saint Peter's triple denial

LORD JESUS CHRIST, Foreseer of the future, I bless and thank you for predicting your most devoted disciple Peter's imminent fall. This was your way of warning him.

I glorify you for enduring Peter's shameful triple denial, by which you were especially dishonored—when in response to a woman's remark, he denied knowing you, saying: *I know not the man.*[1]

I praise and exalt your name forever, for the kind glance you mercifully cast upon blessed Peter, so that when the cock crowed the second time, he immediately acknowledged his guilt, and without wasting time he left the company of wicked men and with much sorrow of heart he wept bitterly for denying you.

Peter did not fall into the deep pit of despair as did the unfortunate Judas, but he trusted in your continuing abundant mercy, which he had often experienced. Thus shedding sorrowful tears, he hastened to do penance, the saving remedy for sin, and found the gate leading to infinite mercy wide open to him.

O the unspeakable love of our Savior! Inexhaustible source of divine mercy and superabundant grace! From this source the sinner draws forth the ardent hope of forgiveness and the

[1] Luke 22:57.

34

just man receives many rich graces. Would that I had a fountain of tears that I too might sincerely bewail my sins with
blessed Peter and through the merits of Christ receive pardon for my sins and regain the graces I have lost.

Overcome by the fear of death, Peter fell and thrice he
denied the truth, but daily I offend Eternal Truth in many
ways and at the least provocation I turn from the way of
virtue. When Peter fell, he quickly rose again; I fall still more
quickly and more slowly do I rise. Rarely do I lament; half-
heartedly do I exercise vigilance over myself, nor do I take
sufficient care in avoiding dangerous occasions of sin.

Peter wept bitterly, and having learned his lesson through
his fall, he fled the occasion of sin. He sought a secret place
to pour forth his tears and with a heart full of sorrow he
washed away the sinful stains contracted by his lamentable
words. Blessed are the tears that quickly wash away past sins
and recover lost graces.

Remember me, Saint Peter, and have compassion on me,
frail sinner that I am, enveloped in so many unruly passions. Do not let the burden of my vices weigh me down,
or let me be carried off by despair for the evil I have committed. You, more than the other saints have greater compassion on those who have fallen, for you know how great
was the mercy the Lord had shown you. Therefore, kind
shepherd, assist the sheep that have strayed, raise up those
fallen into filth, console those who are sad, strengthen the
fainthearted, protect us from the enemy, keep us from falling into his snares, and take the souls of our brothers with
you to the kingdom of heavenly bliss, where you are prince
and porter.

Good and most gentle Jesus, with the sincerest of sighs,
I ask you to look upon me with the same compassionate
eyes as you looked upon Peter after he had denied you. Hasten to grant me the grace of holy repentance to cleanse me

of whatever I have committed against you, whether willingly done or omitted because of negligence. Hear my heart's groans, heal my grief resulting from a bad conscience, and restore to me the light of new grace, for you do not wish a penitent soul to perish, whom you redeemed by enduring so much suffering and shame and in the end the horrible torment of the Cross.

Chapter 9

On Jesus taken from Annas
to the priest Caiaphas

LORD JESUS CHRIST, Priest and Eternal High Priest, I bless and thank you for having been led so shamefully from the house of Annas to that of the high priest Caiaphas, where the scribes and elders had already gathered to take cruel counsel against you. They were all filled with a pathetic joy when they saw you brought in bound before them. On the previous day they desired to seize you but were unable, for your hour had not yet come.

But this is their hour and that of the power of darkness, permitted by God so that they might give vent to their hatred—so long in the making—and openly find an outlet for their deep-rooted malice. All this, so that it be unto your glory, for the salvation of believers and for the eternal damnation of unbelievers as well.

I praise and glorify you, revered Jesus, for standing pitifully before the high priest and the elders of the people, as they brazenly stared upon your amiable face. False witnesses brought accusations against you; you were minutely interrogated by the high priest, you were adjured to tell the truth, calumniated as one guilty of blasphemy, and in the end, and in a loud voice, they all condemned you to death.

I praise and honor you, most noble Jesus, for every insult and lie they hurled against you and for your humble demeanor, which you manifested in your long silence, when bombarded by the many vicious words coming from your accusers. To these you did not respond with grumbling or complaint, but you gave us an example of supreme meekness.

Devout lover of Christ, look with all seriousness on how brightly the excellence of Jesus' patient suffering emanates from him, and witness the offensive disparagements that he, whom the heavenly hosts praise, must endure.

In return for his truthful response, he is accused of blasphemy. But all who say this of Christ are themselves blasphemers and are guilty of a monstrous crime. It is because they do not believe that Jesus is the Son of God that they, in their insanity, indulge in so many iniquitous acts against him. By enduring these attacks in silence and by allowing himself to be trodden under foot by such ungodly men, Christ actually conquers and triumphs.

Therefore, faithful soul, stop complaining about reproaches directed against you and in return do not seek vengeance on your enemies. Rather, bow your head and endure the burden of these temporal trials and seek not to prosper, while Christ chose contempt.

Proud one, blush for your honors, high positions, splendor, and fine clothing, for Christ was poor to the extreme. It is shameful for you to seek favor among men and to desire earthly pleasures, when Christ preferred the contrary.

O adorable Jesus, most meek and kind, grant me, miserable sinner, the desired grace of your favor and teach me by your glowing example not to fear the intimidation or insults of the wicked, nor to be disturbed by false accusations, but willingly to ask pardon for their offences against me. Bowing my head in all humility before you and my superiors, may I receive the gifts of your goodness in greater abundance and return greater thanks to you for graces already received.

Chapter 10

On the insults and mocking that our Lord suffered

LORD JESUS CHRIST, Glory and Honor of the saints, I bless and thank you for the gross disrespect and sacrilegious treatment given you, when, after the sentence of death had been passed, you were disgracefully treated and shamefully mocked by abusive servants. With many a fierce blow they struck you on your head and face.

Your handsome face, upon which the angels gaze with delight, was grievously dishonored by the spittle of your mockers and was struck with heavy blows from their wide open hands. As a result the fresh blood flowing abundantly from your nostrils mingled with the tears streaming from your eyes.

Your pure neck was sorely bruised from the many punches of those striking you. Your eyes, ever so bright and always focused on the just, were blindfolded in mockery, as if you were a fool. Your venerable head, revered above all creatures, was harshly smitten by the corrupt hands of sinners, who scornfully shouted insults, saying: *Prophesy unto us, O Christ, who is it that struck you?*[1]

Lord, who is there that can hear of your multiple injuries and not sigh and feel sorrow in his heart? The suffering you

---

[1] Matthew 26:68.

Christ with hands tied

endured was greater than what any ordinary man could bear, and surely the cruelty of those many insults pierce the loving hearts of the pious. You became a stranger to your friends; you were deserted by those you knew and became the object of your tormentors' mockery and derision. They hated you without cause and winked their eyes at you.

Lord God, Joy of the heavenly court, how could you—as if you were the most foolish of men—allow yourself to be thus mocked, spat upon, and struck by such vile men? Your tormentors, filled with fury, spent that entire night beating and ridiculing you, and by the time they had their fill of punishing you, your face was hardly recognizable. Through all this you maintained an incomparable meekness and matchless modesty of soul that your wicked tormentors were incapable of perceiving. Because you were innocent you suffered all these things out of love and, therefore, you have become dearer and more lovable to all the elect, who, following the interior motions of their soul, acknowledge you as their Supreme Good.

Most patient Jesus, as I reflect on the large number of ignominious insults that you suffered, I ask you to teach me to be aware of my own vileness and, in view of my many sins, to acknowledge that I justly deserve to be despised and ignored by men.

Look with pity on my shortcomings and strengthen my heart that I may put up with abusive words when they are addressed to me. I am well aware of my excesses and my face blushes in shame. Because you were exceedingly humble, you bore, and without murmuring, these insulting remarks for me, despicable sinner that I am. You even suffered chains and stripes.

O how different you and I are; how far I am from true humility! For a slight injury or inconsiderate word, I yield to disliking my fellow man. When I ought to give much thanks for a helpful reproof, I, on the contrary, become sad and grow impatient, thereby gaining nothing by it.

Lord, I beg you, to forgive me for the evil I have done and for frequently offending you by my frivolity. I have not preserved my heart in purity of conscience, nor have I, as I ought, subjected myself with due reverence to you and all rational creatures.

Give me a salutary sorrow together with a fountain of tears. Give me a love for the discipline[2] that I may always recall the blows you suffered. Give me persevering patience to bear bitter accusations and to realize that I am truly worthy of contempt.

May the harsh buffeting of your head inspire me to bear all my bodily sufferings with patience, and may the blindfolding of your eyes restrain the curiosity of my own.

Let the foul spitting on your handsome face repress all carnal affection in me and may it teach me not to yield to this world's external glitter but to appreciate and honor the soul's interior virtues.

May the mockery that you underwent drive from me all frivolous behavior and empty merriment, and may the shameful dishonor shown your dignity extinguish in me all longing for honors and always incline me to what is menial and humble.

---

[2] A discipline is an instrument of penance made of braided or knotted cords. Members of religious congregations used them in chastising themselves.

Chapter 11

On Christ being brought before Pilate

LORD JESUS CHRIST, most just Judge of the living and the dead, I bless and thank you for your hasty and disorderly arraignment before Pilate, the governor. After morning had arrived, with all the chief priests gathered together in one place—their loathsome counsel having been decided to hand you over to death—their attendants took you, at an early hour and under restraint, to the uncircumcised heathen governor. There the most grievous accusations were brought forward against your innocence and you, whom the holy prophets in ages past had proclaimed with high praise as Savior of the world, they called malefactor and destroyer of the nation.

Such horrendous impiety to condemn an innocent person by appealing to false witnesses, to desire the death of the Author of life, to aspire to crucify Christ the King, and to curse one who is holy and just to a most shameful death! May your persecutors be confounded and put to shame. They deserve to suffer worse punishments.

I praise and glorify you, my revered Jesus, for the solemn demeanor and becoming attitude you exhibited while before the tribunal of Pilate the judge. As a meek lamb, bound with cords, you stood in the presence of your accusers— your head lowered, your eyes fixed on the ground, your face calm, speaking but few words and those in a soft voice, awaiting reproaches, and prepared for stripes.

Faithful disciple of Christ, see and consider how your Lord and Savior, King and Judge of all men, allowed himself to be dragged before this judgment seat and how he humbly and willingly subjected himself to secular powers. By this he has given us an admirable example of self-submission, that during community chapter you too may learn to accuse yourself of your many faults and shortcomings and to bear with patience as others censure you.[1]

Submit humbly to your superior's judgment and do not go against those in authority, whom God has set over you. If you wish to avoid the pains of hell, then for the love of Jesus bear patiently all unjust remarks as well as any severe statements made against you. Do not let this wonderful patience of God foolishly slip from your heart when false charges are brought against you. Fall down at the feet of the bound Jesus and beg for pardon and grace. Pray also that he forgive you all your failings, and especially in this time of mercy may he correct your excesses, lest in the future he condemn you forever along with the reprobates.

Have mercy, O good Jesus, have mercy on me, a sinner, for my soul trusts in you. Breathe within me a good spirit that would inflame me to a more fervent pursuit of virtue, and that would lead me to strive humbly and with my whole heart to submit myself to my superiors and to obey all their commands.

---

[1] This refers to a community exercise known as a "chapter of faults", during which a member of the community, guilty of some transgression of the rule, publicly confesses his fault and receives a suitable penance from the abbot. At the same time if another member of the community has noticed a fault in that member, which the latter has failed to mention, then the former mentions it for the latter's benefit. The purpose of this chapter is to guard the religious discipline of the house and to exercise the members in humility and mutual understanding.

Grant me not to fear human judgments nor grudgingly to accept others' accusations, but to desire to be so exercised, accused, and disciplined, and that the growing self-esteem that I find within me be completely trodden underfoot and that my own will be brought to nothing. Thus, by despising myself may my love for you increase and may it ever soar higher and higher.

Chapter 12

On Herod's deriding of our Lord Jesus

LORD JESUS CHRIST, Eternal Wisdom of the Father, Supreme Truth, and Infinite Power of God, I bless and thank you for the shameful contempt and disdain by which Herod and his soldiers ridiculed and mocked you. Herod had for a long time desired to meet you and in his curiosity hoped to witness one of your miracles. But when you declined to answer his questions and to work a sign for him—it was not then the proper time, it was the hour of suffering and not for working signs—he soon yielded to anger and ceased to respect you. Considering you a madman, he dismissed you, ordering that you be clothed in a white garment and sent back to Pilate.

I praise and honor you, my glorious Jesus, for bearing so much fatigue in the weary goings back and forth through Jerusalem's lanes and streets and for being led amid shouts of derision from place to place and from judge to judge. You were everywhere denounced, everywhere dishonored, and after many an interrogation and long examinations, they demanded your crucifixion.

What remarkable patience shined forth in you at this time! Despite all those insults that patience never deserted you. The very thought of your being publicly dishonored engenders repentance in the hard of heart, it pacifies the angry, and invites the devout to weep. You, the Most High God, are here reduced to the lowest of men; you, the All-Powerful, are treated as the most wretched of men; you, the All-Wise, are ridiculed as the most foolish of men; you, the Most Innocent, are judged as the most villainous of men.

Woe to me, unfortunate sinner, weighed down with the heavy burden of sin! Because of my evil deeds I deserve to be assigned to eternal punishment, but you, holy, just, and loving God, chose to be despised and detested to deliver me from the devil's deceits and everlasting death.

I therefore beg you, my good Jesus, whom neither unkind nor unbecoming words were able to disturb, to free me from everything that is outwardly vain and bizarre and that I learn to be content with simple and ordinary attire. It is indeed shameful for earth and ashes to want to be clothed in fine soft garments, while you, King of heaven, were put to ridicule wearing a white garment.

Keep before my eyes the disgrace and scorn you suffered and teach me to follow you in the way of derision and to find joy in contempt. Teach me not to place my trust in the sons of men, or in this world's princes, or in powerful friends, but with my whole heart to despise all earthly delights and those who hanker after them. Lord Jesus, author of my salvation, may I ever follow you with absolute constancy and always keep in mind the many calumnies that you endured for me, unworthy as I am.

Chapter 13

On the angry shouts *Away with him!* and *Crucify him!*

LORD JESUS CHRIST, everlasting Joy of the saints, I bless and thank you for enduring that angry crowd's loud and arrogant cry against you, as the people furiously shouted: *Away with him! Away with him! Crucify him!*[1]

How intense was the rage of that miserable crowd! How inhuman the cruelty of those chief priests and Pharisees! No fear whatsoever could deter them from killing you, and no reason could restrain them from shedding your innocent blood. Though the heathen judge was disposed to show some compassion on your behalf, nevertheless, the hearts of the people were so hardened that they demanded further brutality. Pilate wanted to acquit you and looked for a way to set you free: *I find no cause for death in this man.*[2] The crowd, however, forgetting all the good you had done among them, opposed him, crying out: *If you free this man you are no friend of Caesar. Anyone who makes himself a king is Caesar's rival.*[3]

The people concocted false charges against your humility! Never have you, either in word or deed, sought temporal honors. After the crowd had been fed with a few loaves and

[1] Luke 23:18, 21.
[2] Luke 23:22.
[3] John 19:12.

fishes—an extraordinary miraculous sign—they wanted to make you their king, but you immediately vanished from their midst and sought the quiet of the mountain, where you remained in secret prayer.

Nor were the people content with these lies, for worse things were to be added, namely, their insisting that the judge authorize deicide. The populace cried out: *We have a law, and according to that law he must die because he has made himself the Son of God.* [4] Upon hearing this, the governor became frightened and asked: *Who are you?* [5] And then: *What is truth?* [6] Since the corrupt governor received no answer in reply, and because the crowd doggedly demanded the death sentence, he, seeking the favor of the leaders of the people, yielded to their monstrous villainy and agreed to their unjust request.

How bitterly painful it was when the news of blessed Jesus' condemnation, *Crucify him! Crucify him!* [7] was broadcast throughout Jerusalem. Who, among those who loved him, would not have grieved and mourned when they had heard those cries and shouts advocating that their beloved Lord Jesus be crucified! How mournful and sorrowful was the news the holy Virgin Mary received, when that people's cruel and tumultuous demand for the Cross filled the air.

Grieve, devout servant of Jesus, and from your heart's inner depths bring forth sorrow and repentance. Imagine with what pain the heart of the Mother of God was afflicted, when she heard that her blessed Son was to hang on the despised Cross.

He who always hears the angelic voices resounding in heaven: *Holy, Holy, Holy!* [8] now hears the cursed tongues of

[4] John 19:7.
[5] See John 19:9.
[6] John 18:38.
[7] Luke 23:21.
[8] The author here refers to the *Sanctus* in the Mass; however, see Isaiah 6:3.

the crowd clamoring against him: *Away with him! Away with him! Crucify him!*[9] Only a short time before, on the Feast of Palms, he heard the children praising him with joyful voices, now how times have changed—their parents with depraved spirits want him crucified, saying: *Not this man, but Barabbas!*[10]

You, who love the Lord's Passion, give serious thought to this scene. Close tightly the ears of your heart to this world's unwelcome news, and open them to attend to the sad clamor for Jesus' crucifixion. Faithful soul, I tell you that it would be more to your advantage to focus your mind on this matter than to contemplate the stars in the heavens. If you really love Jesus, you will not pass over this scene without a bitter sigh.

When the world is against you and casts countless insults in your direction, do not let yourself be broken up because of the harsh words and the enemy's threats, rather remember the most patient Jesus and the curses he endured for you, and let all these other arrogant remarks fall on deaf ears. And when your good actions are interpreted as evil and many refuse to accept your word and set themselves in opposition to you, bear all this with meekness; after all, you are not more innocent than Christ, who was insulted with: *Crucify, Crucify him!*

Be aware in advance that as you go along your way to God, you will suffer many contradictions and God will not praise you unless, during your life's various stages, you face trials for his sake. He himself had told his beloved friends: *Blessed will you be when men hate and revile you for the sake of the Son of Man.*[11]

---

[9] John 19:14.
[10] See Luke 23:18.
[11] Luke 6:22.

Follow then the innocent Jesus. While on earth he was rejected by evil men, but was chosen by God the Father and crowned with glory and honor in heaven. Do not allow passing insults to overwhelm you, for God has prepared for you a share in eternal glory.

Lord Jesus Christ, my Friend, in your abundant charity I ask you to enkindle in my heart the grace of genuine compassion for your sufferings. Make me burn with the heat of your immense love, that whatever abuse and insults come my way, I, with peace of mind, may find joy in bearing them and not yield to fear because of the displeasure or taunts of men but with all my heart desire to imitate you in the shame of the Cross.

Strengthen me against my carnal inclinations and grant that I may crucify my harmful passions through effective discipline and with tears to wash away the faults I have previously committed and never deliberately to yield to future attacks of the evil one.

Finally, in every spiritual combat and ordeal of heart I undergo, assist and defend me against the devil's wiles with the strength from your life-giving Cross. May that which was meant to shame you be a remedy for me, and may I return a grateful sacrifice of praise to you for your victory on the holy Cross.

Chapter 14

On the stripping of Jesus and his being bound to the pillar and scourged

LORD JESUS CHRIST, most gentle Protector of all who hope in you, I bless and thank you for your shameful stripping in front of the eyes of your revilers. By command of the impious governor, the praetorium's guards despoiled you of your clothing—you were to die entirely naked on the Cross—they then bound you with rough ropes and finally beat and scourged you with sharp-ended rods, as though you were a vicious revolutionary and a vile malefactor. All this was done to placate the wrathful spirits of the priests, who were intent on destroying your life and on sending you with sorrow to hell.

With humble voice, I especially praise and honor you for being so tightly bound to that hard and cold pillar to free us from the chains of our sins and to restore everlasting freedom to us.

I praise and glorify you with endless gratitude for your barbarous scourging, for every stinging blow and piercing wound to your most holy and tender body. Those savage flagellators mercilessly struck your most pure flesh, tearing deeply into it, adding bruise upon bruise, wound upon wound, with the result that no part of your body remained untouched. Countless streams of your precious blood flowed in abundance from your wounds—like crimson rivulets from a river—to wash us from the long-standing filth of our sins and to cleanse us from all guilt.

Alas, Lord Jesus, how inconceivable the madness of your villainous tormentors! What hearts of stone in those striking you! Though you gave them no cause, they, nevertheless, did not hesitate to scourge you—the most comely of men—and as giants they stood over you and spared you not.

O holy Son, my God's beloved Son, what have you done to deserve such dire treatment? Nothing, of course. But I? I am as one who is lost, for I am the cause of all your sorrows and distress. The enormity of my sins has brought this misery upon you, and to forgive my sins it was necessary for the Son of God to pay by suffering these bitter torments.

Therefore, devout soul, redeemed by Christ's crimson blood, be mindful of the Lord's scourging and in return acknowledge your gratitude to him with a compassionate heart. God's servant in religion, you who live under strict monastic rules, bring this scene frequently before your mind's eye. If you have some difficult task to perform, or if something unexpected happens to your body, all will become light and easy to bear, if you meditate on Jesus' scourging.

Therefore, whenever you are corrected for your shortcomings or chastised for your sins, immediately call to mind the innocent Jesus, stripped of his garments and severely scourged for you and willingly prepare yourself to take the discipline in memory of the Lord's Passion and in expiation for all your sins. Humbly kneel down, remove your scapular, and take off your habit; bend your head and according to the rule submit your whole body to the discipline. Between the salutary strokes, reflect in this manner: "I am ready to receive these stripes for my sins are always before me. Wash me, Lord, from all my iniquity and cleanse me from my sins. Against you only have I sinned and before you have I done evil;

justly do I deserve this discipline." [1] It is better to suffer temporal punishments now and willingly than later to be sent off to everlasting pain. For he who shuns being scourged with Jesus will in the future be excluded from Christ's kingdom as being an unworthy son.

O most adorable Jesus, who endured that most painful scourging for me, the worst of sinners, grant that with a sorrowful heart I may gaze on each of your wounds and kiss them with a deep burning love. From them I breathe the perfume of life and partake of the medicine of eternal salvation. Inflame me with the fire of your infinite love, for you have indeed manifested that love for me—your servant worthy of being condemned—by enduring so many stripes from the scourges in your tormentors' hands. Whenever I am faced with trials, send me your grace to bolster my weakness, lest under the weight of these afflictions I become unduly dejected and agitated, and may I be mindful of your unjust scourging and meekly submit myself to all such ordeals.

Allow me a share in your sufferings and arouse in me the desire to amend my life by taking the discipline, and, being thus humbly chastised, I may present myself as being more pleasing to you in the present life and rejoice with you more gloriously in the next, where all the saints, with all fear of evil gone, rejoice in everlasting contentment.

[1] This is a paraphrase of the first verses of Psalm 51.

Chapter 15

The despoiling, mocking, crowning, and striking of Jesus' head

LORD JESUS CHRIST, glorious King of the saints and radiant Crown of eternal glory, I bless and thank you for the abuse and disgraceful treatment you once more suffered at the hands of sacrilegious men. After the hardhearted soldiers brought you into the judge's quarters, where the entire cohort had gathered, you were shamelessly despoiled of your garments and derisively garbed in a purple robe. This was so that you might clothe us, who are without virtue, with the cloak of your holiness and adorn us with the mantle of your humility.

With singular devotion and a heart full of compassion, I praise and glorify you for the brutal punishment you most patiently suffered in the crowning of your sacred head with thorns—you endured this for us unworthy worms. Your sacred head, the most blessed of all Nazarenes, was covered with thorns that pierced so deeply—even to the inner brain— that copious streams of blood flowed over your ears and neck, eyes and cheeks. As a result, your amiable face, hardly dry from having been spat upon, was disfigured and masked with blood.

What a sorrowful sight to see the Son of God, in whom no sin could be found, so ignominiously and horribly crowned! Because of the soldiers' raging madness, they did

Christ

not in the least tremble as they pierced with many a sharp thorn so holy, so handsome, so noble, and so revered a head. They likewise dared to salute the King of angels by publicly ridiculing, striking, and mocking him.

Most gentle Jesus, King most admirable, Crown of confessors, Strength of the Church Militant, Delight of the Church Triumphant, and Model of all who follow you, how shamefully you were treated, how cruelly tortured! While many a blow was outwardly delivered, you experienced great inward distress, and all this for my sake—to save me from eternal punishment in hell, to cleanse my heart from its vicious habits, and to crown me in heaven with undying glory and honor.

I praise and honor you for the unbecoming welcome and feigned veneration given you, when those ministers of cruelty knelt down before you and violently slapped your face. With contempt did they worship you and with blasphemous tongue did they call you king, crying out: *Hail, King of the Jews.*[1]

Mortal man and servant of sin, consider how much disrespect and anguish the only-begotten Son of the Eternal Father has undergone for you. Open the ears of your mind, and on hearing Pilate's harsh cry *Behold the man!*[2] give way to devout sighs and tears. If you have any feelings of piety within you, let your whole being groan and weep in union with the Creator of the universe.

I praise and bless you, most honored Jesus, for the appalling mockery you endured, when, in order to increase your shame, they put a fragile reed into your right hand as a royal

[1] Mark 15:18.
[2] John 19:5.

scepter—as if you had rashly taken the royal dignity unto yourself.

I praise and exalt you for the violent strokes given your wounded head, when those savage and merciless men, with reed staffs raised on high, fearlessly and frequently struck you on the crown of your head. Once again they spat foul saliva from their mouths and stuck out their vile tongues at you.

Daughters of Jerusalem, come forth and see King Solomon wearing the crown with which his mother, the Synagogue of the Jews, had crowned him on the day of his Passion.[3] Amid what great abuse and insults was he led outside at Pilate's command, so that his wretched appearance could be seen by everyone. In all truth, this is so sad a sight that the thought of it evokes great sorrow. Devout love responds with compassion. The meek and patient Jesus, clad in a purple robe and wearing the crown of thorns on his head, is led from the place of judgment. Perhaps the people, now mad with frenzy, will be somewhat moved to compassion when they see him so dishonored and afflicted. Alas, the crowd's raging fury becomes more intense and when the governor cries out, *Behold the man!* they shout back still more shockingly: *Away with him! Away with him! Crucify him!*[4]

Faithful lover of Jesus, having heard and taken all this to heart, tremble and blanch at the enormity of his sorrows. Strike your breast, shed your tears, and kneel down at the sight of the crowned Jesus, dressed as a king but in truth

[3] This passage was most probably suggested by a sermon of St. Bernard, part of which was incorporated in the old Roman Breviary as Lesson IV of the Second Nocturne of the first Friday in Lent (Office in Memory of the Coronation of Our Lord Jesus Christ with Thorns). See *The Roman Breviary Reformed by Order of the Holy Ecumenical Council of Trent*, second volume (spring), translated by John, Marquess of Bute (Edinburgh and London: William Blackwood and Sons, 1908), p. 220.

[4] John 19:6.

filled with shame as the most despicable of slaves. He endured the horror of these wretched punishments to draw you from all desire for worldly glory and to extinguish in you the disease of pride.

You, who are but the slime of the earth, ought to be ashamed to hanker after worldly glory, when you see your Lord's most noble head so disgraced. As a member of that thorn-crowned head, you ought to be stricken with grief when you see him, who is of supreme majesty, preferring what is lowly and painful. Do not desire to seek an easier way of life, rather, with fervor follow the more austere way.

All you sons of pride, who strive for higher places and carry your heads on high in your desire to appear better than others, be engulfed in shame because you are much worse. Blush in embarrassment, you who go parading in the presence of the scourged and thorn-crowned Jesus, arrayed as you are in silks and precious stones, with your bodies, which are soon to die, bedecked with gold and silver jewelry, and your heads handsomely and ostentatiously attired. At the same time you give no thought to the work of your redemption nor to the fact that you were redeemed by such dire suffering.

Take comfort, take comfort, poor ulcer-covered Lazarus, and you, whoever you may be, who according to this world's standards are considered worthless, for despite your infirmities and shortcomings you bear a greater resemblance to Jesus of Nazareth than does the rich man, who, arrayed in purple and fine linen, continues in his evil ways.

And you, cowled monk,[5] do not be ashamed if the habit you wear is of coarse cloth and patched, because then—if you are

---

[5] The cowl is the hood attached to a monk's habit. The cowled monk, then, is distinguished from those members of the community, who, though they have been vested with the habit, have not as yet received the cowl.

shabbily dressed, but handsomely clothed in holiness—you will have special glory before God and his angels. May great shame be yours, O monk, if you should desire a habit made of finer cloth. You ought to be dead to the world and, furthermore, you have chosen to practice poverty in all its ways.

A religious may become downcast because of his afflictions, but if he frequently meditates on Jesus' most cruel crowning he is certain to find true and comforting solace. If you find yourself filled with anxiety, recall the many thorns that Jesus endured, and you will—and with greater calm—bear whatever annoyances may come from others, even severe headaches, and what is usually the most troublesome, the sharp thorns of calumny and slander.

It is to your greater advantage to suffer with the suffering Jesus and to wear a crown of thorns with the crowned Jesus, as you now endure many nuisances on this earth of ours. However, if you live solely according to your own desires, you will later have to suffer hell's punishments as well as the most acute torment of the damned, namely, to be eternally separated from the adorable face of Jesus, our Savior, and to be excluded from the delightful company of the blessed. He who is not ashamed to have a share in his reproaches and the sufferings he endured in his Passion, will, at the time of the dreadful Judgment, stand fearlessly and joyfully before his Eternal King.

How pleasing and dear to God is that soul, and how fruitful will his meditations be, in which he inwardly suffers the pains of Jesus' Passion, is wounded to the heart by his wounds, and by reflecting on his death experiences a love-death with him.

Good Jesus, ever meek and patient, I lament over you, so severely scourged, so disgracefully mocked, and most barbarously crowned for me. That I may grieve still more deeply, I ask for the grace of a sorrow that penetrates my entire being.

I humbly prostrate myself before you and adore your exalted majesty, so contemptuously treated in your human nature. With lips dedicated to your praise, I heartily beseech you to imprint clearly and stamp indelibly on my heart that mournful countenance that was yours at the hour when everyone rejected you as a loathsome leper, and you, wearing a crown of thorns, were hurriedly led outside as a spectacle to the waiting crowd.

May this most sorrowful image of you penetrate the innermost areas of my heart and may it so afflict and distress me that all that is worldly and curious disappear before my eyes and that all that is carnal and lustful perish within me. May all that is bitter and vile become sweet and pleasing because of you, and may the contemplation of your sufferings stamp out my evil inclinations and the thought of your heavy sorrow allay my daily anxieties.

May this holy image of your crowning, earnestly and profoundly meditated upon, be a great comfort to me in time of adversity and may it strengthen me against the mind's lustful wanderings. When a person's mind is occupied with divine realities and is given to penitential practices, he is both free of all harmful thoughts and is protected from the enemy's piercing shafts.

Cleanse me, Lord Jesus, from the contagion of material possessions. Clothe me with true virtue and grant me to rejoice when I meet with contempt. When I find myself deprived of necessities, may I bear this with meekness, and when old garments are given me rather than new or when something shabby is offered me rather than something of quality, let me not be offended. Let me not complain about those who laugh at me, or argue with those who reproach me, but by my remembering your crown of thorns may I calmly accept, for the sake of my salvation, whatever pain and affliction may come my way.

Finally, pierce my hard heart with the sharpest thorn in your head and embed it in my heart's very center so that all my body's noxious blood may flow out through the wound it makes, and may that goad of your holy love remain fixed therein until I am fully purged from the thorns of vice and thistles of temptation and have prepared myself to become the seedbed of virtue. Then may the soil of my heart, once infected as a result of the primal curse, receive a new blessing by the infusion of your sacred blood, and may there bloom the rose of charity rather than the thorn of envy, the lily of chastity rather than the nettles of lust, the violet of humility rather than the burr of vanity, and the blossom of gentleness rather than the bramble of impatience.

Chapter 16

On the unjust condemnation
of Jesus to death

LORD JESUS CHRIST, Author of life and Standard of justice, I bless and thank you for your unjust condemnation to
death—without any offense on your part—while a murder-
ous revolutionary, unworthy of life, was spared. How detest-
able a decision; how contemptible an exchange!

Because a tremendous tumult had arisen among the people, in no way was the judge able to appease that crowd's
madness. He returned to his judgment seat and there pronounced his infamous judgment against you, namely, that
the thief Barabbas, who was worthy of death for having committed a capital crime, was to be released, while you, who
were free of all offense, were to be punished with a most
shameful death—being handed over to be crucified.

Such, alas, is this world's judgment! To what lengths is justice eviscerated when the ungodly are in command! Behold
how the Just One perishes and there is none to free him.
The One who is true is given over to the fraudulent, and the
Holy One is scourged by the unholy. The Innocent is handed
over rather than the guilty; a thief is chosen over Christ, and
Barabbas is released from his bonds in place of Jesus of Nazareth. The Lamb is exchanged for a wolf, a saint for a criminal, the best for the worst, a desperado acquitted rather than

true God. Darkness is preferred to light, vice to virtue, death to life, scum to gold, shell to pearl, and he who is infamous is favored over him who is noble.

Who will not grieve when he hears these things? Who will not become inflamed against that crowd? Who will not speak out against that judge? He may wash his hands and excuse himself before men, saying that he acted out of fear of Caesar, but he was constrained by that crowd's insistence. He is not totally free from guilt, however, for he knew that Jesus had been handed over to him out of envy.

Indeed it would have been better for him to have lost all temporal power and honors than to have condemned one who was innocent and whom he knew to be just. It would have been more profitable for him to have lost everything in this world than to sin against God by killing the Christ.

How terrible will the judgment on the last day be for the unholy and unbelieving, when God the Judge, who is now judged to be unjust, will appear in the glory of his majesty. All the devout faithful, who deeply mourn the sacrilegious condemnation of Jesus Christ, their Lord, will then rejoice, and all who patiently bear the afflictions of this world and suffer its injuries and contempt will on that day be joyful and feel secure.

Holy and loving Lord, unjustly judged by Pilate, the governor, and condemned to the ignominy of the Cross, grant that during the community's chapter of faults I may humbly accept any decision made against me, and may I not foolishly judge my superior or attack my accusers with injurious remarks, but following the example of your patience may I imitate your virtuous silence. Nor let me take offense when trampled upon by someone placed over me, but let me leave all judgment to you.

The servant is not greater than his master. If you, who are the judge of all, were so poorly judged, and since you, who

were totally without guilt, offered no resistance to your violent enemies, how much more I, who often and in so many
ways have been at fault, ought to submit to the censure of
my fellow monks. Help me, most kind Jesus, cheerfully to
bear the yoke of submission and the rod of correction, and
whenever afflictions come my way, may I always remember
your sorrows.

Christ Carrying the Cross

Chapter 17

On Jesus' carrying his Cross and being led to the place known as Calvary

LORD JESUS CHRIST, true Vine, Way of life, and our Salvation, I bless and thank you for carrying your heavy and ignominious Cross before all those bystanders. Patiently and humbly you bore it for the redemption of the entire human race, that you might carry on your shoulders the long-sought and after-much-difficulty-found lost sheep to your heavenly home.

I praise and honor you, eminent Standard Bearer of the Christian army, for your sad and pitiful treatment, when that heavy wooden Cross was cruelly placed upon you, and when you were shamefully led through that renowned city, where earlier you had made yourself known by your preaching and miracles. At the time when the crowd's fury and bitterness grew more and more intense against you, you were condemned to be suspended from the tallest Cross between two despicable men, as if you were a common thief or a leader of brigands.

Wonderful Jesus, I praise and glorify you for your difficult and troublesome setting out on that most unusual journey, which you undertook for us. I praise you for each and every step you took on your way, for the great weariness your body felt—already weakened by torture—and for the hardship you endured in going up and down that winding road under the burden of your Cross. I praise you for your being forced forward and being treated roughly by those who had charge over you—when you were told to move ahead, they either cruelly pushed you from behind or pulled you forward from the front. You were manhandled in every way. Bent over and weighed down under that insupportable burden, you made your way to the place called Calvary. Never before had you made such a journey! Never before had you walked so rough a road! Never before had you carried such a yoke!

I praise and highly exalt you for your being so greatly despised by those vile men, leading, dragging, and insulting you. I praise you for the many disrespectful words hurled against you as you made your way, for the lying and derogatory remarks made against your innocence, and for the rude rejoicing of your enemies looking forward to your cruel death and their arrogant joy in awaiting your shameful crucifixion.

Amid all these horrors you meekly went on as a lamb on its way to sacrifice, all the while thinking of our salvation, grieving over the blindness of your people, and deploring the wickedness of those prodding you onward.

I praise and bless you for the heartfelt love shown by your friends, who shed abundant and compassionate tears on your behalf, and for the devoted following of the sorrowing women, who wept bitterly and followed your every step with heads bowed low. Turning toward them, you assuaged their mournful sobs with these comforting words: *Daughters of Jerusalem, do not weep for me, rather weep for yourselves and your children. If they do this in the green wood, what will they do in the dry?*[1]

How great the mourning of all your dear ones, especially the lamentation of the holy women, who, since they were

---

[1] Luke 23:28, 31.

unable to get near enough to comfort you or to save you from so terrible a death, kept looking upon you with profound feelings of compassion.

How overwhelming the sorrow that claimed the maternal feelings of the Virgin Mary and caused her to tremble, when she saw her beloved and only Son with the Cross on his back and being led to his death! How willingly your Blessed Mother, the most loving Virgin Mary, would have endured the shame of the Cross if she had been permitted to take your place, and how quickly she would have chosen to die in your stead if she knew this would have been acceptable to you. What she could not bear in her body—nor was she permitted to—she mentally bore and this most profoundly. Because her love was so ardent, her sorrow was greater and her affliction more severe; in a true sense she carried the Cross with you.

Into the hearts of none of those who loved you, did your sorrow so penetrate as into the loving soul of your Virgin Mother, endowed as she was with such exceptional love. Nor is there any doubt that Mary Magdalen, who loved you with a most fervent love—though almost enfeebled because of her profuse shedding of tears—would have, because of an onrush of love, willingly taken hold of your Cross together with your Virgin Mother and gladly carried it in your place.

In addition to the sufferings that you endured from exterior causes, your interior anguish of soul was compounded by the defection of your disciples, your Mother's sorrow, the anxiety of those who had given up hope in your Resurrection, as well as the fact that your suffering proved a stumbling block to many. While the faith of many individuals was shaken or lost, the sole exception was that of the glorious Virgin.

Disciple of Christ and fellow religious, if you wish to attain the joys of heaven, then hasten to carry the mystical Cross and be determined to walk in the steps of your Redeemer.

Do not be put off by heavy but short-lived penances, nor desire a relaxation in the observance of religious discipline, rather view as easy and light all that your institute requires and joyfully fulfill all that holy obedience asks of you.

If you find it difficult to obey every order given you, then know that Christ has fulfilled for your sake even weightier orders, namely, death on the despised Cross. Therefore, be faithful in following the strict rule of our fathers and do not swerve from the path that leads to the kingdom. Have nothing to do with roadways that are smooth, for they are designed to draw the slothful to a foul end.

On the day you entered religion, you accepted your cross, and on the day you professed your vows you bound yourself still more closely to it. Imitate the Crucified by living a holy and righteous life. If you want to increase your religious fervor, then carry your cross with gladness. If you complain and bear it unwillingly, you will not receive the glory Jesus has reserved for you, but the punishment of the unbelieving thief. If, on the other hand, you endure all things with joy and meekness, then you have in great part overcome the evil one.

Therefore, do not fear the rigors of religious life, nor count as long your days within it, for the love of Christ and the joy of a well-lived life can transform irksome chores into happy tasks. There is one who went before you and who lived a much more difficult life, namely, Jesus, the Son of God and great patron of the Cross, who himself experienced the Cross' heavy weight. Therefore, follow your Savior in the way of the Cross; by not abandoning the religious life nor relaxing the resolves of any fervent monk, you will be safe forever.

If you wished to enjoy this world's delights or to remain in command of your possessions or to follow your own desires, you would then have remained in the world. By your entrance into religion you chose to walk with Christ, hence observe the rule you have promised to follow. Ask

Jesus to assist you mightily, for he, who had inspired you at the outset to begin well, will see that you successfully complete it.

My beloved Jesus, Prince of this earth's kings, Ruler of angels, and eminent Standard Bearer of all Christians, you carried before that deriding crowd the Cross on your own shoulders for your servants' salvation and, as an example to them, now assist me in my hesitation to follow you in that sad procession. Do not abandon me before the appointed time of my death and afterward lead my soul, liberated from this body of sin, to Mount Calvary, the mount of myrrh and frankincense, where you were crucified and died for me, so that I may find security beneath the sign of the Cross and there rest in you.

Grant me to start again but with new fervor and to follow you, not with the fickleness of those who are lukewarm, but with the eyes of my heart ever fixed on you as you carry your Cross, I may avoid the wavering of the inconstant. Be a guide to me as I travel along the narrow road and be my companion on the way, a helper in good times and a consoler in times of adversity, as well as a partner in the many labors that I have taken on for your name's sake. Help me to bear the day's heat and burden and that I may join my community in singing the liturgical hours and assist at the holy services. Grant also that in moments of stress and great anxiety that I may call to mind your extreme weariness under the heavy weight of the Cross and, thus, the slight burdens that I must bear will become insignificant when I consider the weight of your heavy Cross.

Relying on your kind assistance, I will freely and willingly endure the rigors of religious life, into which I have entered, and though you may permit me to feel its weight for a brief period of time—so that I may grow in humility—you will, at the proper time and in the proper manner, eventually come to my aid by manifesting your mercy to me.

Teach me to conquer my will, to be satisfied with few things in life, and not to desire to journey outside the monastery. Let my hands be occupied with work and my heart taken up with meditating on the Holy Scriptures; let the members of my body be employed in serving you, my senses kept under strict control, and may I, insignificant as I am, be numbered among the true cross-bearers.

Remove from me all interest in worldly matters and put an end to all attachments to the flesh. Let me not find delight in others' affairs, or waste time in useless chatter, but strive to concentrate on my interior life and to grieve and lament secretly over my many excesses and negligences. May I reject all that keeps me from advancing in virtue, and may I follow the path of those who keep their eyes focused on you—those who with a calm spirit know how to transcend all temporal things.

Diligently will I call to mind the Cross you so lovingly bore for my sake, and may I in turn be inflamed with the love of the Cross so that I may daily give myself to you by being obedient to my religious rule. Finally, may I willingly and without any show of resistance bear the burdens laid upon me, until the time I arrive at the long-desired place of peace and safety.

Chapter 18

On the crucifixion of the Lord Jesus and his hanging naked, high, and long on the Cross

LORD JESUS CHRIST, most gracious Creator of man and Restorer of his wounded nature, I bless and thank you for being so rudely despoiled of your clothing as you stood before the Cross, where, in the view of the crowd— roaring like animals waiting to pounce on their prey— you were stripped and left naked. Your clothing, harshly torn from your body, was given to them as their prize. You stood there shaking and ashamed, with only a piece of thin linen cloth to cover your loins and a wreath of thorns as your crown. You were the reproach of men and the object of their derision. You stood there like an outcast and poor pilgrim, without any of this world's goods, the poorest of the poor, totally destitute and without human comfort.

As the first Adam walked about naked in paradise prior to his fall, so in like manner naked you ascended your Cross to restore that lost paradise, from which Adam, because of his sin, was expelled and driven away. In order that that lost innocence be restored to him and that he again be clothed in the robes of virtue and be worthy of eternal life, you allowed your own clothing to be stripped from you, and yourself to

be overwhelmed by sorrow and confusion and finally to suffer a most bitter death.

I praise and glorify you for your ever-consuming love for
our salvation, for your being so violently stretched out on
the hard wood of the Cross, waiting there to receive you. I
praise you for the pungent piercing of your hands and feet
and the hammering of stubborn nails into them—the sound
of which could easily be heard at a distance and surely capable of moving the hard-hearted spectators to tears.

So forcibly were you nailed to the Cross that your body's
veins suddenly burst open and streams of your precious blood
flowed freely from your various wounds. So harshly were
you stretched, both lengthwise and in breadth—similar to
the skin membrane on a drum—that all the joints in your
body gave way and your every bone could be counted. You
allowed your hands and feet to be transfixed by evil men,
and in this way your sacred hands, while nailed to the Cross,
paid back the heavy debt incurred by Adam, who had extended his deadly hands to the forbidden tree. By your precious blood you wiped away that long-standing debt.

I praise and honor you for being raised on high and for
hanging for so long a time on your Cross—a piece of wood
despised and cursed by your own people but highly honored
by all Christians as the most blessed of trees growing in the
forests. You hung there for our salvation, for three long hours
or more and, thus, you won those marvelous graces of the
Cross, which would prove especially beneficial to the whole
world.

You were lifted high above the earth so that you could
draw the hearts of the pious faithful to you, lest they float
aimlessly among degrading pleasures, and to render the loving hearts of those devoted to you to feel greater compassion
for you. By seeing you on your Cross, their great love for
you would only grow more intense. You were lifted on high so

that you could visibly and definitively triumph over the powers of the air, and so that you could earnestly pray for sinners and offer full forgiveness to all who are truly penitent. Likewise, so that your death may bring peace and harmony to all in heaven and on earth and, thus, make all things new again.

O faithful servant of Jesus, raise your eyes upward and with a sad heart and grieving face look upon your God and Redeemer hanging between the lofty arms of the Cross. Your Beloved is naked and he wants you to look upon him. Because his feet are fixed by nails, he awaits your coming and desires you to approach freely. He stretches out his most loving arms to you; he shows you his open wounds; he bends his head to kiss you; he is prepared to receive you in his favor and without any hesitation to forgive you your every sin.

Be brave, therefore, and calmly approach his Cross, touch the figure thereon lovingly, embrace it warmly, hold it firmly, and kiss it devoutly. Prostrate yourself before it and lie there hugging that sacred ground. Remain there so that at least one drop of his blood might fall upon you, or that you might hear the words he speaks from the Cross or be present when his agony comes to an end. May the very earth that received the dying Jesus also receive you, and where Jesus was buried, may that very place also be your resting place. Since you are now one with him in spirit, may you also be one in your body's burial.

Mourn for him as you ought and enter the secret chambers of your heart. May the Crucified find you a sorrowing and dedicated disciple, one who is grateful and devout, totally his, and lovingly drawn to his wounds. May it be said that the entire world is crucified to you and you to the world and that for you to live is Christ and to die with him your greatest gain.

Far be it for you to glory in anything but the Cross of your Lord Jesus Christ! Far be it from you to depend on your own merits, for your entire salvation and redemption is in the Cross of Jesus, and only in him should you firmly place all your hope. It is through him that there is remission of sin. From him flows the treasury of merit and with him are the rewards of the just, which he will render according to each one's deserts.

Therefore, follow the example of the Crucified by setting aside the burdens of this world and by withdrawing your heart from all that can harm your interior freedom. Distance yourself from all disturbing phantasms and earthly cares, and live with pure unadorned truth. Hold yourself in contempt and despise all transitory material goods so that you may sincerely and truly imitate the naked Lord on his Cross, and in view of your ardent love for your suffering Redeemer, that you may bear the slanders and insults of men. In this way you yourself may become worthy and gain sufficient strength to mount your own cross.

Learn to rejoice when others despise and ignore you. Mourn more deeply over others' misdeeds and pray that everyone strive to be better. Look upon yourself as one worthy of contempt and sincerely desire that your enemies be saved. Do not place too much trust in men. There are few who, in the time of need, prove faithful, and loyal friends are rare. Do not be surprised at this nor take it amiss. Christ knew what it was to be deserted by friends and to be surrounded by enemies. He, who always did good to others, received gross ingratitude in return.

Put your trust in the Crucified, our only worthy guide and teacher. Remain close to him on his Cross, and you will enjoy his assistance during times of trial and will be given the palm of victory over all who harass you. Prepare a place for him, and by sincere repentance and humility make yourself ready to receive God's grace. May you receive and relish sweet comfort from Jesus' sufferings and wounds, and may you know how pleasant it is to suffer insults and to be accounted as nothing, all for his holy name.

Choose a solitary way of life, cut off from all sources of distraction; seek comfort in the Cross, resist sensuality, avoid committing small faults, refrain from quickly yielding to idle chatter, keep silence in affairs that do not concern you, and be careful to preserve your interior blessings.

It hardly becomes one who is dedicated to the Passion to break out into riotous laughter, and it is less in keeping with religious decorum to exhibit a lack of gravity in one's behavior. One can learn all this from Christ's Passion, and blessed is he who lives his daily life accordingly; he will advance more quickly than his brethren and will eat of the fruit of the tree of life, wherein he will find joy without end.

Most Holy Father, look upon the face of your Christ, hanging on the Cross for me, and in view of your only-begotten Son's exceptional merits, his being pierced with nails and being covered with his own red blood, be merciful to me a sinner, bound and chained as I am to my many sins. He was wounded to wipe away my iniquities, and he will offer you satisfaction for all my sins and will answer to you in my stead. I offer him to you as a hostage; I choose him as my advocate; I assign him as my mediator; I designate him as defender of my cause. If acceptable to you, he, the blessed fruit of the Virgin's womb, will make good all my omissions and rectify all my past commissions.

Most merciful Father, you will hear him with wondrous sweetness, and in view of his singular love and great desire for my eternal salvation, may I experience this hope and consolation as something most helpful to me in this present life and as necessary after death.

O good and gentle Jesus, beloved Son of God, in following your Father's will you deigned to take unto yourself the

substance of our flesh—without the stain of sin—and to offer it on the altar of the Cross for the world's salvation. Have
mercy on me, your servant, who now asks your forgiveness
and grace. Relying on your goodness and the infinite merits
of your Passion, pardon all my sins committed against you,
whether recent or old, knowingly or unknowingly. Your merits far exceed mankind's wickedness and your abounding
atonement is much greater than all my iniquity, no matter
how frequently committed. Knowing this, I come before you
under the protection of the Cross and hope for still greater
mercy. From the depths of my heart I ask and seek the remedy that will bring me to salvation.

I revere the sign of the Cross; I honor the banner of the
Cross; I kiss the foot of the Cross; and I beg judgment from
the Cross. Hear me, wretch that I am; receive me a fugitive;
heal my contrite heart; justify me a sinner. I will not leave
you nor depart from you until I am again in your favor.

I beseech you, my crucified Lord Jesus, free my soul from
all love for the things of this world. With your arms draw me
upward to the height of the Cross; let me follow you wherever you lead. Raised high above all worldly concerns, I will
be near and close to you, and as an exile in the world I willingly join with you in being poor, naked, and unknown.

Instill in my flesh a fear of you, lest I yield to carnal ap-
petites; pierce my hands, lest I yield to sloth; transfix my feet
that I may remain firm and courageously endure toil and
sorrows. May your nails enter my heart's center and there
inflict a saving wound, as a consequence of which and because of my overwhelming contrition, may I shed tears and
be lost in love of you. Fill me with grief and increase my
devotion, until nothing will be more pleasant or dearer to
my heart than Jesus Christ and him crucified.

Chapter 19

On Jesus' wounds and the shedding of his precious blood

LORD JESUS CHRIST, Author of our salvation and most gracious Dispenser of pardon, and most patient in tolerating man's wickedness, I bless and thank you for the great pain, the many stripes, and the bloody wounds inflicted on your tender and noble body. From the soles of your feet to the crown of your head there was no area without its injury or lesion—either swellings or smarting wounds—with warm red blood flowing over your body.

I praise and glorify you with the greatest reverence of which I am capable and with full interior humility, for the abundant shedding of your precious blood from your five sacred wounds as well as the other wounds, both great and small. In bleeding they give forth the most effective medicine for our sins, more precious than balm.

Most gentle Jesus, you were so mistreated and manhandled by cruel men that you had no bodily strength left in you. Your veins were opened wide—not even the least drop of blood remained in you, and whatever of that sacred fluid had been in you in life has now in death been poured out for our souls' benefit as the price of our salvation.

O five precious wounds, supreme signs of incomparable love, abounding with divine sweetness, it is from you that the sinner learns abiding trust—otherwise his guilty

conscience would cause him to despair. In these wounds
we find the medicine for life, abundant grace, full forgiveness, unstinting mercy, and the gateway to promised glory.
Whatever defilement I incur or whatever sins of the flesh I
commit, it is in these five fountains that I wash myself clean,
am purified, and again made new.

I praise and honor you, Christ, only beloved Spouse of
the Holy Church, for your uncommon charity, by which
you chose, through this covenant in your blood, to redeem
my soul from the effects of Adam's transgression, to cleanse
it of all sin, to enrich and adorn it with the merits of your
holiness. Sanctified by your grace, may I be found worthy of
being united to you and later of being blessed in your glorious kingdom of light.

Faithful soul, attend carefully and see with what great and
noble a price he has ransomed you—he, who out of his own
gracious goodness created you in his image and likeness. You
were redeemed from Adam's sin as well as your own many
sins, which you willingly and knowingly committed, and this
not by anything corruptible like silver or gold, but by the
precious blood of the immaculate Lamb, Jesus Christ. He
shed his blood on the Cross not only for your cleansing, but
also that he might leave that same blood in a chalice for you
to drink with deep faith, when you partake of the sacrament
of Communion, through which the sins of the world are
daily purged and washed away.

How grave will be the punishment of him, who considers
the sacrament of the Son of God's covenant as something
unworthy, and does not offer suitable gratitude to the Crucified's wounds! Strive, therefore, to give thanks to so great
a lover and generous a benefactor, at least by offering a short
prayer or by making a brief meditation sometime during the
day or night. Many faithful souls, aflame with love of him,

have gladly shed their blood for him, and many others, sharing in his sufferings by following the hard path of penance, have offered the bitter waters of contrition in exchange for the chalice of his blood.

Learn from their example to crucify your flesh with all its desires and vices, to resist temptation manfully and to bear the yoke of voluntary obedience until death. On the altar of your heart, offer to Christ your Redeemer the sacrifice of a contrite spirit rather than a martyrdom in blood. By serious meditation call to mind the benefits that come from the Cross and in the depths of Jesus' wounds seek, as in the clefts of a rock, a place of refuge from the face of your enemy and those pursuing you.

Most kind Jesus, come to my aid in all my needs and in every difficult moment. Stretch out your hands over me and with your right arm protect me always. Instill devotion in my heart, put truth on my lips, and grant me strength in my labors. Cleanse me from sin's corruption and by your precious blood heal my wounds.

Let nothing dark remain within me, nothing impure or what can defile me, but may your sacred blood, that was shed so abundantly, cleanse me of everything harmful and sanctify all that I do. May my spirit and soul, for whose redemption you, my Creator, endured so many cruel sufferings and paid such a price from your inestimable treasury, be presented to you, at the final judgment, pure and undefiled.

Chapter 20

On Jesus' prayer for his enemies

LORD JESUS CHRIST, Fountain of holiness and sweetness, I bless and thank you for your abundant love and heartfelt prayer for your enemies and for those crucifying you. With hands outstretched on the Cross, you pleaded for them, asking that they be pardoned, and you generously excused their transgressions, saying: *Father, forgive them for they know not what they do.* [1] Indeed, these are words, full of grace and sweetness, capable of softening the hard heart of any sinner and of moving him to repentance!

O sweet Jesus, how inclined you are to forgive, how easily appeased, and how eager to show mercy. Great and boundless is your kindness, Lord, to all who love you; you likewise manifested that same loving kindness toward your enemies. Hanging high on your Cross you were not moved by any bitterness against those crucifying you, nor did you seek vengeance on those tormenting you. You did not pray for the earth to swallow them up, or for fire to come down from heaven and consume them that very instant. Rather, like a welcome rain, you uttered sweet and loving words on behalf of your cruel tormentors, saying: *Father, forgive them, for they know not what they do.*

[1] Luke 23:34.

These words reveal your most excellent love as well as your indescribable meekness, qualities that could never be obliterated in you. Nor were you held back from uttering a prayer. Your executioners shouted: *Crucify! Crucify!*[2] and you responded with the words: *Father, forgive them.* They drove rough nails into your body and you offered excuses for their unheard-of wickedness, saying: *They know not what they do.* O Christ, how wonderful is your love!

The perversity of such obstinate men, incapable of being moved to repentance by such loving words! You grieved more because of their blindness with regard to the evil they were doing than for the injuries done you. The heinousness of their actions pained you more than all the wounds they inflicted on you. They abused you as much as they could, and in return you rendered them whatever good you were capable of showing them. The most generous and best thing you could do for so wicked a group of men was to pray that they turn from their malicious deeds and acknowledge you as God's true Son, who came in the flesh. In this way Isaiah's memorable words, spoken of you in years gone by, were fulfilled: *And he bore the sins of many and has prayed for his transgressors*[3] that they may not perish.

Who of us can now despair about not having his sins forgiven, when they, who crucified the Dispenser of pardon, experienced such abounding kindness? My soul, though you may be guilty of many crimes, do not despair. You may be caught in the web of your evil passions and may be subject to many severe temptations, nevertheless, disheartened one, you still have the hope of life. The bowels of mercy are

---

[2] John 19:6.
[3] See Isaiah 53:12.

available to you, and the Cross, nails, lance, and Jesus' many blood-covered wounds are witnesses of that mercy.

Penetrate deeply into the five sacred wounds of the Crucified, kiss his other wounds, cling to the tree of life with loving arms, and hold fast to Jesus hanging on his Cross, for he is the certain pledge of our salvation. Worship him devoutly, commit yourself to him with full faith, and abandon yourself completely into his hands. Since he had shown himself to be good and merciful to his enemies, then he will certainly be more gracious to one who sorrows over his sins.

If you, however, wish your prayer to be heard the sooner, and if you desire to win your Redeemer's grace and obtain the fullness of his mercy, then from the depths of your heart forgive your brother for whatever he has done against you. Forgive him in small matters so that God may forgive you your more serious offenses, and pray for his salvation in the same way as you pray for your own. You will find grace and, by imitating the example of Jesus, who orders us to love our enemies and to pray for our persecutors, you will become the child of the Most High.

If you train yourself to forgive all injuries done you, even though you suffer them unjustly, and to pray for those who have wronged you, then you have gained for yourself at the hour of your death a confident hope. Such holy prayer for one's enemies has won eternal blessedness for the apostles, has glorified the martyrs, ennobled the confessors, adorned the virgins, and made all the saints like unto Christ and deserving of eternal life.

Most gracious Lord Jesus, I ask you, who in your vast love deigned to pray for your enemies, to pray with that same love for me to the Father that he grant me full pardon for all my sins and mercifully free me from the punishment I deserve for them. Grant me a firm and abiding trust in your love, that I yield not to despair because of the greatness of my sins, rather that I remember that you have come into this world to save sinners and that it was your will to suffer, to be crucified, and to die for the sinful.

Therefore, may your prayer on the Cross, uttered on behalf of your enemies, be also for my soul's salvation, and may it grant me great hope of pardon, which, through your most holy intercession, I may be judged worthy of receiving, for in no way can I obtain it on my own merits. Grant that I may freely and safely find refuge under the shadow of your wings and may the standard of your holy and invincible Cross protect me from all fear of the age-old enemy.

As I cling to your Cross, I beseech you to stretch out the branches of your arms over me, for at whatever hour my poor and sorrowful soul may be called from this world, grant that it be free of fear and know not despair, and that you receive me, poor sinner, for I rely totally on your mercy and not on my own accomplishments.

Chapter 21

On the disrobing and dividing
of Christ's garments

LORD JESUS CHRIST, Creator of all things and Giver of
all good things, I bless and thank you for enduring your violent disrobing and, amid mockery, the ripping off of your
clothing. After being nailed to your Cross, you were cruelly
despoiled of all your clothes, leaving you dispossessed even
to the last scrap of cloth. You were even left without the
smallest piece of cloth to cover your nakedness, nor was there
enough linen left to serve as a winding sheet, in which your
dead body could be wrapped and decently buried. If you
were not to be buried naked, then a shroud would have to
be procured from another party and given to you out of charity, as to one both poor and destitute.

O the great consuming greed of those soldiers—not soldiers, but dishonorable riffraff! O the disgraceful rapacity of
those degenerate guards, who, overcome by ungodly avarice, were not ashamed to tear off Jesus' few belongings and
greedily add his meager garments to their booty. They separated his clothes into four piles, each soldier receiving his
share, but the seamless robe alone was left untouched. For
this, they cast lots—it could not be divided and at the same
time keep its form. Those unfortunate despoilers and hateful
malefactors had not the slightest pity on the poor, naked

Jesus, hanging there. They neither returned to him the tiniest piece of cloth, nor did they leave his fringed robe as a comforting remembrance to his sorrowing mother. They did none of these things, but being devil-inspired and fearless of future judgment, they continued in their outrageous sacrilege.

My beloved Jesus, you neither say nor do anything against these actions of theirs, rather you suffer them in silence. By doing without your clothes you clearly indicate what I must do when something I deem necessary is taken from me. You want me to be prepared to prefer temporal losses rather than to seek whatever is legitimately due me. I presume that the texture of your garments was not especially fine, nor were they cheerfully colored, but that they were plain and simple, very similar to what this world's poor wear. Or perhaps, they were simply made according to the style of the people of Nazareth or after that of the ancient prophets. They certainly were not the work of any expert tailor, but were sewn together with a needle in the hands of the Blessed Virgin, under the inspiration of the Holy Spirit. Or perhaps the Virgin Mother purchased them for her Son during his days of childhood, with money earned from the work she did for her neighbors.

O great Creator of heaven, true God and true Man, that you should be reduced to this extreme state! At the time of your birth, you scarcely had the poorest rags to cover yourself, and now at death you have lost all your clothing! Previously a narrow manger held an infant's tender body, now stripped of all your goods there is no place in this world, which you created, for you to rest your head except on the Cross. You came into this world as one poor and in need and you now desire to leave it naked and as an outcast. At your birth your body was tightly wrapped in swaddling clothes, now at death that body is pierced by nails and a lance.

To meditate on such great affliction arouses compassion in us and to witness such great endurance invites us to imitation. Therefore, show more patience when something you consider a necessity has been taken from you, or when what you deeply desire is denied you. If you learn to live with little and be content with what is mean and lowly, then you will be free of all complaining and you will enjoy great peace of mind and be acceptable to almighty God.

Who will give me a small piece of my Lord Jesus' sacred garments or permit me to touch them with a devout heart or to kiss them with my lips—for from these there flowed forth great power to heal the sick. Indeed, holy are the relics of those garments and with what great reverence are they preserved, wherever they are found.

If the soldiers had truly known the excellence of those garments, then in their greed they never would have cut them up nor would they have sold them for some paltry sum, but with the greatest of care and with fitting reverence they would have preserved them in silver chests. Certainly these relics are more precious than all the mantles of kings and bishops' fillets, and, furthermore, there is no precious metal worthy of being compared to them. But the holiness and reverence due these relics were hidden from those irreligious men, and because of their desire to satisfy their gluttonous avarice, they were incapable of perceiving the fragrance of their excellence.

It is indeed deplorable that so august a treasure should be thus disgracefully destroyed by men playing dice. I should think that if one of Christ's wealthy, powerful, and faithful followers were there at the time, he would have willingly offered a great sum of money to redeem those sacred relics or would have acquired at least some part of them for himself and, enriched with such a prize, would have returned to his home amid great rejoicing.

Now, sweet Jesus, patient endurer of a multitude of indignities, grant that I may, for your greater praise and glory, be able with a devout mind to undo the tangled web that those infamous soldiers have woven for your sorrow. Blessed is that holy and immaculate garment which for many a year clothed your most pure body, born of the Virgin Mary. Blessed is the edge of that garment, for we read that when the sick approached you and devoutly touched it, they were instantaneously healed. Blessed is your seamless robe, not to be worn by any human, but worthy of sacred use by God alone.

It was fitting that that robe should remain whole, not only because of the special reverence due it, but that it might also proclaim the unity of Holy Mother Church throughout the world. Though the Church is divided by reason of regions, languages, and cities and is diverse because of different classes of men in varying occupations; nevertheless, the entire body of the Church exists, is governed, and is conserved under one head and one supreme pastor. The Church professes one faith, ministers one baptism, believes in one Triune God, has one Spouse in Jesus Christ, now reigning in heaven, and from whom it can never be separated, no matter what the temptation might be. Lord, this is because you gave your bride, the Catholic Church, the impregnable shield against all errors, namely, the word of truth, the light of knowledge and the fervor of charity, that she might thus attain the never-fading crown of eternal life.

Lord Jesus, you are the poorest and the richest of kings: the poorest because you were stripped of your clothing and deserted by friends; the richest because the fullness of all spiritual gifts resides in you. Grant your poor servant that I may perfectly attain to at least one virtue from among your many virtues, namely, that before your eyes I may never be found to be naked and ashamed, similar to him, who, while attending the marriage banquet was found without his

wedding garment, and for that fault was immediately expelled from the fellowship of the saints.

Whenever I recall the fourfold dividing of your garments,
may my heart be torn by a salutary sorrow for my sins; may
it be moved to this either by the fear of hell, the hope of
future glory, sorrow for past sins, or loving gratitude for graces
received.

Grant me, as your seamless garment is its sign, to preserve
the unity of brotherly love in the bond of peace and, for the
love of interior peace, to reject all that may lead to dissen-
sion. May I avoid the bustle of this world, abstain from wan-
dering about, and engaging in useless gossip, and may I desire
to lead a pure and hidden life with you. Let me not crave
worldly happiness or want to own things. While you were
on this earth you possessed no worldly goods, and the little
that you seemed to use to fulfill your needs, even this you
permitted the despoilers to take from you and disperse. In
this manner you give an example of patience to all who suffer wrongs done to them, lest they yield to inordinate sadness over the loss of their belongings.

Chapter 22

On the crowd's insults and Jesus' enduring perseverance on the Cross

LORD JESUS CHRIST, Glory and Joy of the heavenly court, I bless and thank you for the many insults and blasphemies that that infamous crowd hurled against you while you hung on the Cross. Everyone there was against you—from the oldest to the youngest. Like mad dogs they huddled together to attack your innocence. With their mouths they barked like dogs, they gnashed their teeth like lions, and with their tongues they hissed like snakes. They cursed with their lips and their faces they turned into sneers; they clapped with their hands, their feet danced, and their hearts rejoiced, all because they saw you nailed to a Cross—one whom they did not want to see die without first being mocked and jeered. Those who passed by shook their heads like crazed, drunken men, and filled with bitterness, arrogance, and ill will, they shouted: *Ah, there's the man who destroys God's Temple and rebuilds it in three days.*[1]

The chief priests together with the scribes and elders, who appeared to have had the crowd under their control, should have restrained the people from such malice, but, in fact, they were more shameless in insulting you than were the others. Opposite the Cross they stood; with pride-filled eyes

[1] See Mark 15:29.

and necks erect they brazenly stared you in the face. Laughing among themselves, they spat forth their unseemly blasphemies, saying: *He saved others; himself he cannot save.* [2] In this way they attempted to distort and disparage your divinely-worked miracles as well as your cures and healings. You had done all these out of kindness for others, and because of them they were known to be jealous.

They likewise urged you to come down from the Cross and though on many occasions they had already shown themselves hostile to all who believed in you as the Christ, they now falsely declare their willingness to believe in you. When you worked your more outstanding miracles, they never put any faith in you, but conceived further calumnies. They never intended to believe you or to seek salvation; their only desire was to aggravate you by derisive remarks. Bursting with defiance, they finally hurled impious words against your divinity, and with hatred in their voice they addressed you as the Son of God: *"He trusted in God, let God deliver him, if he will; for he said, 'I am the Son of God.'"* [3]

O most cruel and brutal persecutors of the Son of God! Were you not satisfied with being the cause of this shameful crime of crucifixion, that you should now add to your horrifying sins those of blaspheming and ridiculing the Son of God? Alas, what are you doing? Why do you sharpen your venom-filled tongues against one so holy and innocent? In what way has Christ sinned, or in what way has he ever injured you?

Has he not done all things well—he who made the deaf to hear and the mute to speak? Did he not bring fame to your whole nation by his many extraordinary miracles, as

[2] Mark 15:31.
[3] Matthew 27:43.

well as by his most appealing doctrine? And did he not pray
for his enemies? What evil does he deserve for these good
deeds of his? Why do you return evil for good and hatred for
love? It would be more fitting for you to weep in order to
expiate so great a crime than to give in to laughter in the
presence of the Crucified!

In hearts so obstinately closed, there was no compassion,
contrition, or remembrance of benefits received. But the
devil-inspired madness within them—ever ready to utter more
biting barbs and insults—urged them on to more heinous
deeds. Now that they were no longer able to torment him
with swords and clubs, they resorted to sharper weapons,
namely, their tongues.

In similar fashion, the soldiers, ignorant of God's laws and
responsible for carrying out this sacrilegious deed, found pleasure in fulfilling their duty, and, abetted by the encouragement and goading of their officers, they approached the Cross
to mock you. Offering you vinegar, they said: *If you are the
king of the Jews, then save yourself.*[4]

O dull-witted soldiers, corrupt both in your actions and in
your morals, who has instructed you to wage war in such a
manner that you battle against God? It is not the practice
of valiant men to persecute one who is good or to despoil
a poor man or to leave naked a man that had been robbed;
nor is it to rend another's clothing or to make jest of the
Crucified or to offer vinegar—which no man enjoys
drinking—to God, when he is about to die. No matter
how much you try, you cannot cause harm to Christ, for
wisdom overcomes malice and Jesus' patience can in no
way be eroded.

[4] Luke 23:37.

Similarly, the thief on your left, obdurate in his depravity, remarked in like fashion: *If you are the Christ, save yourself and us.*[5] What a wretched man! Yielding to contempt he plunged headlong into the pit of iniquity, and, rather than seeking forgiveness for his past sinful deeds, as he ought to have done, he shamelessly insulted you, from whom all forgiveness flows. Consequently, that unhappy man died miserably, with despair in his heart.

Lord, I praise and glorify your steadfastness and perseverance in remaining on the Cross you embraced, and from which neither flattery nor empty promises could induce you to descend—not for one brief moment would you have abandoned that which you had willingly ascended. It was your firm decision to remain unto the end and to die on the Cross you had chosen with so holy a love; likewise it was always your desire to bring to a glorious end the work of salvation that you had initiated. You, who taught others to persevere in doing good works, manifested your obedience by remaining on the Cross, and, by that example of yours, you indicated to your followers that they too must show constancy in being obedient.

You, who are a professed religious, who despise the world and are a lover of the holy Cross, approach nearer to the tree whereon the Crucified hangs. Show yourself a man and remain steadfast in your holy resolves. To be a member of our Order, to live under obedience, and to persevere in religious discipline is not only doing the work of Christ, but it is also the way for you to achieve your salvation. Therefore, let no one talk you into leaving the religious state or entice you away from the path of perfection or keep you from engaging in pious conversations or from keeping the vows you professed.

[5] Luke 23:39.

Remember the Apostle's words: *Christ became obedient for us unto death, even to death on the cross.*[6] Therefore, whatever the world may promise you or whatever may appeal to your body, no matter how severely the devil may tempt you or friends try to dissuade you, or even if the world laughs at you, pay no attention to all these, but ignore and scorn them.

Stand firm in Christ; look upward, focus your eyes on the Crucified, who with wide open arms invites you and promises you, for a short period of toil, an eternal reward. He says: *If you will suffer with me, you shall reign with me; and if you will die with me, you shall be glorified with me.*[7]

O Jesus Christ, most valiant and invincible Champion, most ardent Lover and Consecrator of the holy Cross, now that I have accepted to live in religion, grant me to continue to serve you willingly and let not the tedium of work weaken my fervent desire to imitate you.

Impel me always to move forward and with a firm will to resist the temptations of the flesh and to strive for victory in spiritual trials. Let me exercise great patience when times prove difficult and not fear the ridicule of men or seek their praise. Turn my eyes from all that is of this world, and let me seek you, who are my sole refuge and only salvation.

Let me not withdraw from the embrace of your holy Cross because of someone who may be dear to me or one not to my liking, but under its protection and with it as my emblem and standard, may my life, because I have been obedient, meet with a happy end.

---

[6] This is actually an antiphon taken from the Office of Holy Week, but it is based on Philippians 2:8.

[7] This is more or less a conflation of two texts in St. Paul, Romans 8:17 and 2 Timothy 2:12.

Chapter 23

On the words spoken to the thief
on the Cross

LORD JESUS CHRIST, sole and supreme Comfort of sinners, I bless and thank you for the immeasurable kindness and infinite mercy you manifested to the thief hanging on the cross to your right—once a despicable man but now a sincere penitent and a disciple. At the very moment that he acknowledged his sinfulness and genuinely repented of his evil deeds, he was granted, in view of the promise that you had given him, remission of all his sins as well as access to paradise. Where there is wholehearted contrition and total conversion, repentance, even if it be late in coming, does have its beneficent effects.

Indeed holy and salutary is that conversion and contrition for sins by which one merits to enter the kingdom of heaven! The penitent thief—now a blessed confessor—though he had sinned seriously over a long period of time, nevertheless, at the end and in his greatest need, came to his senses, and being sorry for all his past deeds humbly asked forgiveness. Abundant mercy was shown him in return. In declaring that he was rightly condemned to death, he at the same time acknowledged his own culpability. When he reproved his comrade in crime for his unseemly blasphemy, he showed his love of justice, and, in remarking that Christ was crucified without cause because he was free of all fault, he manifested his compassionate nature. The man, who does not despair of God's mercy but asks to be remembered in God's kingdom, indeed has remarkable faith!

Endowed with such virtuous qualities, the thief, as he hung on his cross, saw his entire life pass before him and so with total confidence he turned to you, Lord Jesus, our caring Shepherd of souls, our true Priest, and most faithful of Confessors, saying: *Lord, remember me when you come into your kingdom.*[1]

Most kind Jesus, you answered him in return with the sweetest and most comforting of words: *Amen I say to you, this day you will be with me in paradise.*[2] These words, flowing so graciously from God's lips are indeed sweet and endearing, but to the ears of a contrite sinner, as he undergoes his agony in his final hour, they are far more gracious for they bring immense comfort to an anxious and fearful heart. He who is privileged to hear such a promise can die in total confidence. The individual, for whom God agrees to be his defense, has nothing to fear on Judgment Day.

What was denied to Peter, after he had made his request, was granted to this self-confessed thief. Peter desired to remain on the mount of contemplation[3] but his petition was not granted. Before the hour of Christ's Passion had come, Peter had expressed his desire to follow Jesus wherever it would take him, but he was told: *You cannot follow me now, you will follow me later.*[4] Peter was among the first to be called as an apostle, but the thief enters the kingdom before him.

[1] Luke 23:42.

[2] Luke 23:43.

[3] This was Mount Tabor, where our Lord was transfigured and where Peter asked permission to build three booths, so that Christ and his two heavenly visitors could prolong their stay (Luke 9:33).

[4] See John 13:36.

How wonderful are your works, Lord; your thoughts are exceedingly deep; inscrutable are your judgments; indescribable the words of your mouth. For one who is unwise, these matters are beyond him, but they far surpass the understanding of a fool.

How fortunate was the thief to suffer one hour with you, to die with you, and then to proceed with you into your kingdom. I know not what good he may have done earlier in his life, but of this I am certain, that when his end was approaching, he was cleansed of all his evil deeds and this because of his humble confession.

This then was the greatest of mercies, that one so villainous should be pardoned as quickly and as soon as he poured forth his deeply felt prayer to you: *Lord, remember me when you come into your kingdom.* Gracious and merciful Lord, as soon as you heard this prayer as you hung on your Cross, you immediately comforted his sorrow-filled heart by responding so kindly: *Amen, I say to you, this day you will be with me in paradise.*

It would indeed be both salutary and consoling for me to reflect and meditate on the thief's death and your most compassionate response. Not that I may sin the more boldly, nor to postpone my repentance any longer, but not to yield to despair if suddenly I should become ill, now that I know that so sinful a man as the thief had been so quickly converted and by your merciful grace was granted eternal salvation and admitted into paradise.

Because of my countless sins, I should indeed be alarmed if I had no knowledge of your mercies, Lord, and if I had not heard of penitents whom you had most generously received back. Through the prophet you have spoken: *I do not desire the death of the sinner, but that he turn from his sin and live,*[5] as

[5] Ezekiel 33:11.

well as with your own lips: *God so loved the world that he gave his only begotten son that all who believe in him will not die but have eternal life.*[6] And again: *I did not come to call the righteous, but sinners.*[7]

Without any delay you forgave Mary Magdalen's many sins, as she wept copious tears at your feet. And Peter, after he had three times denied you and had cried bitterly, you again took into your fellowship. In your mercy you restored to health those afflicted with various diseases and because of your abundant love you freed those held captive by their serious sins. This is clear in the case of the adulteress, whom you snatched from the clutches of her accusers and delivered from being stoned.

O lovable Jesus, my mercy and my refuge, who protect and deliver me from the wrath of my enemies, be merciful to me and let not my soul perish among the ungodly, for it was precisely in order to redeem my soul that you voluntarily suffered your crucifixion.

Recall the sacred words you directed to the thief, for by these very same words you have offered me unfailing hope. O my life's Savior, when the hour of my death approaches, say to my soul: *This day you will be with me in paradise.* For a dying man there are no more joyful or sweeter sounding words to be heard than your most gratifying response: *This day you will be with me in paradise.*

Lord, remember me in your kingdom. Do not abandon me at death's fearful moment, when my strength begins to leave me, when my voice becomes only a whisper, when my sight grows dim and my hearing almost nil. At that moment, good Jesus, come to my aid; send your holy angels to comfort me in my agony and may the hateful enemy, who subtly

[6] John 3:16.
[7] Matthew 9:13.

awaits my final hour, not prevail over me. At one time this same enemy dared to detect some weakness in you, which he would then try to use to his advantage, but finding none, he departed completely nonplused. May those who seek to destroy my soul be confounded; let them be turned away and swiftly put to shame.

Lord, let my soul rejoice in you and find joy in your salvation, as I reflect on your most consoling words, your second utterance from the Cross, *Amen I say to you, this day you will be with me in paradise.* May these words, more tender because they came from you as you hung on your Cross, be often on my lips and still more often in my heart. Words addressed to me from the lips of my crucified Lord are most endearing and eloquent, and for this reason they merit more serious attention and profound reflection.

Would that I so live and serve my Lord that at the hour when I leave my body behind, I may be worthy to hear those gracious words from heaven: *This day you will be with me in paradise.* If only you would speak those other heartwarming words to your servant: *Well done, good servant, because you were faithful in small matters, enter the joy of your lord.* [8] Nothing would then be better or more gratifying than to have lived a good life and to have served you faithfully until death.

---

[8] Matthew 25:21.

Chapter 24

On the extraordinary inscription
with the name of Jesus
and placed above his head

LORD JESUS CHRIST, almighty Prince and King of all creatures, I bless and thank you for that extraordinary inscription bearing your holy and blessed name, boldly displayed above your head. Governor Pilate had it clearly written in the three best known languages of the world, that is, Hebrew, Latin, and Greek. This was the form that those words had: *Jesus of Nazareth, King of the Jews.*[1]

That inscription was indeed extraordinary. It was not the result of human inventiveness, rather it came about by divine decree, foreseen and foreordained from all eternity. Pilate, therefore, ought not, nor could have written in any other way than as you inspired him to write. The mystical meaning of that inscription, as expressed in those words, has its foundation in the celebrated books of the prophets. What Sacred Scripture had clearly predicted in years gone by and what tradition has consistently taught in praise of your grace-giving name, the gentile governor, under divine inspiration, inscribed on a small wooden tablet as an everlasting memorial of the Crucified: *Jesus of Nazareth, King of the Jews.*

[1] John 19:19.

Since many in the crowd had read this inscription, the priests—their jealousy ever on the increase—could no longer tolerate that the glory of your name be proclaimed abroad, and so with all their cunning they tried to bring disgrace upon it and, what is still greater madness, tried to eradicate both your name and your life. For this reason they took the matter up with Governor Pilate, saying: *Do not write, King of the Jews, but that he said I am King of the Jews.*[2] Their fear was that they would become involved and that the cruel crime of crucifying their own nation's king would be laid at their door. In order that such a claim spread no farther, they requested that the inscription be changed so that it would not appear that you, Jesus, were crucified as a result of their malice, but rather because of your presumption in assuming royal status for yourself. In fact, while you were in this world you never took unto yourself any royal dignity.

O you wicked people! The truth is not as you try to make it out to be, for in every way you yourselves are the guilty ones. You are the principal murderers of the Son of God. You are without excuse, and with artful cunning you seek to mask this horrid crime. In Pilate's very presence you disavowed the Holy and Just One and asked that a man guilty of murder be released to you. You have advanced to this point, that you now dilute the truth of the inscription so that you yourselves may appear without guilt.

With regard to the Lord's death, Pilate was much more innocent than you, and in writing this inscription he was more truthful, and in responding to your envy-filled request, he was more constant, saying: *What I have written, I have written.*[3] He equivalently said: "If you care to read it,

---

[2] See John 19:21.
[3] John 19:22.

then read it as it is, otherwise forget about it. Once I have come to a decision you will not turn me from it. What I have written, I have written. I did not seek your advice in writing this inscription, nor will I change it just because you request it. It will remain as I have ordered it. It was inspired by God and not by man. Therefore I confirm it and proclaim its truth and I maintain that nothing will convince me to change it. By it, I make known his dignity to all peoples and in all tongues, and I order it to be broadcast abroad that Jesus of Nazareth is the King of the Jews."

O noble Governor, you wrote well and you responded correctly. I praise you because you had prepared so holy and handsome an inscription for Jesus of Nazareth, and because you had silenced the priests. However, I do not praise you for giving your consent to Christ's death, for in doing so you have committed an unspeakable crime.

And you, devout disciple of Jesus, learn carefully to ponder the words of this holy inscription, read them reflectively, and pronounce them reverently, for the very reading of these words, *Jesus of Nazareth, King of the Jews*, is a powerful shield against fear of the enemy. Make the sign of the Cross, touching your forehead and then your breast and devoutly repeat the words of the inscription, and instead of experiencing fear and anxiety you will feel that greater strength is yours. By calling upon Jesus' life-giving name, *Jesus of Nazareth, King of the Jews*, neither your firm faith in God nor the power of Christ will permit your salvation to be endangered. No words can fully express, nor can any mind adequately comprehend the sweetness of this most worthy inscription. It has but few words, but these draw the entire world to venerate the holy name. O all you princes, tribes, and peoples of the world, hear, read, and proclaim: "Hail, Jesus of Nazareth, the King of the Jews, who has suffered for the salvation of all peoples."

O Jesus of Nazareth, glorious offspring of the Virgin Mary, renowned son of David, only-begotten of the Most High Father, write your sweet and excellent name clearly and firmly on the tablet of my heart, and together with it that holy and honored inscription giving the cause of your death, so that I may keep it ever before me and frequently read it in praise of your venerable name.

May that inscription bring comfort to my heart when I am distressed, and may it be my singular protection when severely tempted. And whenever I read or think of the words, *Jesus of Nazareth, King of the Jews,* may the evil spirit depart from me, may my burning concupiscence die within me, and may the whole world be as bitterness to me.

Indeed, there is nothing sweeter than Jesus, nothing more beneficial, nothing more valuable. No one is brighter, or purer, or more holy than the Nazarene. Nor is there anyone more worthy than the King of the Jews, or more powerful, or more exalted. Therefore, Jesus, whenever I humbly invoke your name, or recall your passion, or pronounce or reflect on the words, *Jesus of Nazareth, King of the Jews* let no enemy challenge me, no plague touch me, no disaster destroy me.

O Jesus, you are eminently lovable, you are my King and God, my delight and beyond all my praise. You were lovable in your manger, more lovable on your Cross, and most lovable as you sit on your throne in your kingdom. Though you underwent your crucifixion in the weakness of your flesh, nevertheless, you now live by the power of God and sit at the Father's right hand, exalted above all creatures for ever and ever. Amen.

Chapter 25

On our Lord's compassion for his sorrowful Mother and his giving of the Blessed Mary and Saint John to each other

LORD JESUS CHRIST, Consoler of all who mourn, I bless and thank you for the sad scene you witnessed when you gazed upon your beloved Mother standing at the foot of your Cross, overcome with grief. You best knew how great was her sorrow, for you alone fathomed the most secret depths of her heart. While you were on this earth there was none dearer to you than your Virgin Mother, and there was none she cherished more than you, her Son and God. Though born of her, she still acknowledged you as the Creator and Lord of all things. Therefore, when she saw you, whom she loved so thoroughly, hanging on the Cross, her thoughts were all on you rather than on herself. As if drawn out of herself and lifted on high, she also, in spirit, was crucified with you, though in body she remained standing and weeping at the foot of the Cross.

I praise and glorify you for your infinite compassion, with which you, as a loving Son, grieved with your most sorrowful Mother. She took upon herself all your sorrows as if they were her own and wept over each of your wounds as though they were hers. Furthermore, whenever her motherly eyes saw blood flowing from your body, or when she heard your voice speaking to her from the Cross, she suffered ever new torments.

I praise and honor you for your most tender words that you finally addressed to your grief-stricken mother, commending her to your beloved disciple, John, who was to be her devoted guardian. By the indissoluble bond of love, you joined Virgin with virgin, saying: *Mother, behold your son,*[1] and then to the disciple, *Behold your mother.*[2]

O blessed union and gracious commendation brought about and consecrated by virginal integrity! By your words, you manifested your filial and loving care for your Mother's honor and assured her of protection in the person of your chaste disciple. You offered him to her as another son, as if to take your place, and being pure he would fit in well with her manner of life and would see that she was provided with life's necessities. It was your devotion as a loving son that prompted you to do this, namely, that the spotless Virgin, your holy Mother, would not be without a faithful companion. Inasmuch as she would be deprived of your sweet presence, she would feel left alone in the world, a stranger among her own people.

Holy Mother of God, may your Son's holy desire and excellent commendation please you, and may you graciously welcome this disciple, whom your Son Jesus has chosen for you. He is John, one of the apostles, a virgin, someone special, more beloved than the others, refined in demeanor, cordial in speech, bashful in countenance, modest in behavior, temperate in food, simple in dress, conscientious, and ever ready to obey. He is the most beloved disciple, a relative of

[1] John 19:26.
[2] John 19:27.

yours, and enjoys a good reputation; he is pure in mind, chaste in body, pleasing to God, respected by everyone, and well worthy to be your companion, O Mother of God.

I well know that whatever pleased your Son has also pleased you and continues to please you, and I also know that it is your supreme desire to do what he wished done, for in all his actions he never sought to do his own will but always sought his Father's glory. Therefore, I have no doubt that it pleases you that as he was about to leave you, he wanted John to take his place with you.

Holy John, accept the priceless treasure offered you. Receive the Blessed Virgin, the revered Mother of Jesus, Queen of heaven, Mistress of the world, your beloved aunt and your mother's sister. Until now the Blessed Virgin Mary was looked upon as your aunt because of a blood relationship, but because of a special grace now offered to you, she is to be called your mother, and this by a more sacred bond and by divine choice. And you, who, according to the flesh, were once known as the son of Zebedee, the brother of James the Greater, relative of the Lord our Savior, and afterward one of Jesus' disciples, shall now be known by a new name, Mary's adopted son, and with a son's love you shall obey her in all things. Therefore, do as Christ bids you; fulfill his sacred commendation and you will be honored and beloved by all.

Blessed John did as Jesus bade him from the Cross. For from that very hour the disciple received her into his own home; he watched over her, carefully attended to her needs, diligently obeyed her, and loved her with all his heart.

Rejoice and be glad, Blessed John, because of the charge entrusted to your care. Christ confidently handed over to you what he deemed his dearest possession in this world. And when he, as his final testament, bequeathed to you Mary, whose praise the holy angels cannot sufficiently sing, he showed you his special favor. Christ may have given Saint Peter the keys of the kingdom of heaven, but he appointed you his own Mother's chamberlain. Mary was once betrothed to Saint Joseph, but now she is commended to you, who are to be her second protector. The angel addressed Saint Joseph saying: *Do not be afraid to take Mary as your wife,*[3] but the Lord of angels now says to you: *Behold your mother!*

Just as Saint Joseph did not fail in his duty to the Virgin at the time when their Son was born, neither did you fail your Mother during the hour of Christ's Passion nor during the long span of years after his ascension into heaven.

If Blessed John the Baptist were alive then, it would have rightfully seemed to me that, since he was both a close relative of hers and was known for his chastity—he would have been a most suitable protector and would well fill the role of the bridegroom's friend. But since Saint Joseph was not then alive—nothing else is actually known about him, whether he survived or had died, and John had been executed after a long imprisonment, and Jesus himself was about to die and soon to be taken from his mother's gaze—it is for you to take the place of these dear ones and to be a son to her instead of Christ, who had been taken from her.

I trust in the Lord Jesus that your brother James and the other apostles will heartily agree with this arrangement, that none of your friends will envy you, and that those who are close to you will rejoice with you. You deserved this extraordinary reward because of your many virtues: your total contempt for this world, your love for Jesus, your pleasant manners, spotless purity, evenness of mind, openness of soul, inviolable conscience, and probity of life. Therefore, take Christ's Mother under your care and abundant grace will be yours in return. From being with her, you will be uplifted

<hr />

[3] Matthew 1:21.

and will benefit much: you will find instruction in her words, edification in her example, assistance in her prayers, and inspiration in her admonitions. Her charity will inflame you and her devoutness encourage you; you will reach new heights in meditation, be filled with joy, relish spiritual consolation, and savor heavenly delights.

From her lips you will hear divine mysteries and will be taught things hidden until now, you will witness marvels and comprehend what is now beyond comprehension. By being in her very presence, you will become more chaste and will remain wholly pure, you will grow more holy and your devotion will ever increase.

Her very appearance is purity, her words prudence, her every action justice, her reading Jesus, her meditation Christ, her contemplation God. Her graceful countenance radiates light, her face is awe-inspiring yet it turns no one away, her delicateness purifies those who look upon her, and her speech drives away all evil.

Such is Mary's dignity and so great is it that it surpasses all the saints in purity and grace, and by the Most High King of heaven you have been appointed to be her companion. Therefore, fulfill your office diligently, show her due honor, and surround her with your loving care.

Now stand next to the Cross and watch at Mary's side; with your arms embrace her when she feels weak, support her when she feels faint, and comfort her when she sheds tears. Weep with her when she weeps, grieve with her when she grieves, move with her as she moves, stand when she stands, and sit when she sits. Do not leave her alone in her sorrow, but remain and fulfill this work of mercy.

Since Jesus is about to die, prepare yourself for his burial. Take his Mother with you to the sepulcher, return to the city, lead her to your home, and comfort her, who is the Comforter of the Afflicted. Be as a ministering angel to her, though in this instance you offer comfort to one far more worthy than you. Christ was comforted by an angel at the time of his agony and though he did not require it, nevertheless, he did not refuse it because he chose to be ministered to by an inferior.

Behold, dearest John, to what sacred office you have been called, as well as the Virgin who has been committed to you and whose Mother it is that has been given to your care.

I now humbly ask you, offer a fervent prayer for me a sinner, that I may also grow fervent in my love for Jesus, be found faithful in praising the Blessed Virgin, and in sharing in her sorrow.

Chapter 26

On the admirable virtues of the Blessed Virgin and on her sorrow and tears

O VIRGIN MARY, Mother of God, I bless, praise, and glorify you for all the gifts and good things that God has so bounteously bestowed upon you, for your untold virtues, as well as for your extraordinary privileges of grace. Because of these you clearly outshone all the saints on earth, so as to be considered worthy of becoming the Mother of God, of holding in your lap the Word of God who was born of you, embracing him in your holy arms, lifting him up, and carrying him about.

I bless, praise, and honor you, humble handmaid and chosen Mother of God, for all the love filled care you showered on Christ, your Son according to the flesh, as well as for the assistance you offered him whenever he needed it; likewise for the misunderstandings, poverty, labor, and fatigue you so peacefully endured with him.

I bless, praise, and exalt you, August Virgin, Mother and Daughter of the Eternal King, for the many enjoyable conversations you had with Jesus, for carefully listening to the holy words as they came from his lips—these you diligently kept within your immaculate breast and lovingly meditated on them in your heart—and for the unheard-of consolations you so frequently received from him, for the extreme joy and great delight that over the years you so happily experienced by being in his presence, as well as for the inspirations with which the Holy Spirit enlightened you.

I bless, praise, and acclaim you, Holy Mary, my honored Lady, for your most holy and pure life, so pleasing to God and to the angels, and for the many years you spent with Jesus in solitude and great poverty, during which you endured various trials and afflictions. Thus you set an example for all Christ's disciples faithfully to follow and which will be of benefit to the universal Church, as she suffers diverse misfortunes until the end of time.

I bless, praise, and extol you, Mary, most gentle and devoted Mother of God, for your holy meditations on God's law and all the pious exercises you practiced both day and night; for your most fervent prayers, tears, and fastings, ardently offered to God for the conversion of sinners and the perseverance of the just; for your heartfelt compassion toward the poor and the sick, and toward those tempted and suffering anxiety; for your overwhelming desire for the salvation of the human race, which would be redeemed, as you knew, by your Son's bitter death.

Though it was with an indescribable love that you loved your only Son, nevertheless, you did not keep him from advancing toward that hated Cross, rather you submitted yourself totally, together with your Son, to the divine will. You suffered with Jesus in all his pain, and courageously you followed in his footsteps as he made his way to the Cross. You gave no thought to flight as the disciples had earlier done, nor did you fear the anger of the crowd, for you were prepared to undergo death with your Son, rather than abandon him at this most difficult time.

I bless, praise, and magnify you, heavenly Mary, most faithful and lovable Mother of God, for persevering in your firm faith and perfect love, while several of the apostles fled from fear and some others followed him, but these did so out of shame. With the inextinguishable light of faith that was yours, you alone never doubted, during your Son's Passion, that after three days he would rise, as he himself had so clearly stated. Though all of Jesus' friends had scattered, you, most sorrowful Mother, made your way with a small group of women through the raging crowd, and hastened to Mount Calvary in order to be as near as possible to your son, who was about to be nailed to his Cross, there to look upon him while still alive, and where, shortly before his death, you would hear him recommend you into John's care.

I bless, praise, and highly commend you, holy and immaculate Virgin Mary, for taking your sorrowful station at the foot of Jesus' Cross, where you stood for a long time careworn and afflicted, transfixed by the sword of sorrow, as foretold by Simeon; for your many tears, which you abundantly shed; for the great loyalty and unwavering allegiance you manifested to your dying Son in his most dire moment; for the acute heartbreak you felt the instant he died; for your tear-filled countenance when you saw him hanging dead before your eyes; for your blessed embrace when in your Mother's arms you received him from the Cross and amid laments clasped him to your breast; for your dolorous journey to the sepulcher, walking behind those who bore that sacred corpse and seeing it placed in a tomb with a large stone sealing it; for your rueful return from the tomb and your entering your home where many of the faithful had gathered, and there you again bitterly bewailed the death of your loving Son. Inasmuch as everyone's eyes were upon you, they too broke out into tears.

My soul, suffer with the sorrowful Virgin, the weeping Mother, the loving Mary! If you love Mary, then share in her great sorrow, so that she might come to your assistance when you yourself are burdened with trials. Look how the holy Mother weeps for her only Son, how Mary Clopas weeps for her dearest nephew, how Mary Magdalen weeps for the physician of her soul, how John weeps for his beloved Master, and how all the apostles weep because their Lord has been taken from them. When so many friends are weeping, who would not weep along with them? Indeed, there was great lamentation in Jerusalem that day!

Therefore, you too should stand for a time next to the Virgin Mother and learn from her, whose bitter tears are capable of penetrating the depths of your heart, what it is to lament. Overcome with unheard-of sorrows, she now stands next to the Cross, but at an earlier time she stood next to a manger, her soul filled with heavenly music. She is now bombarded with the insulting shouts of the crowd, but previously she was attuned to the comforting voices of angels. She is now clad in the cloak of mourning, but earlier she received the homage of holy kings.

The red blood of her Son, whose glowing cheeks she used to kiss ever so tenderly, now drips upon her; she now sees him hanging between thieves, but not very long ago she witnessed the countless miracles he performed on behalf of his people. Because he is covered with open wounds, he resembles a leper, many of whose bodies he miraculously restored to their original wholeness. She looks upon him crushed under so much pain, and it was he who delivered the sick from their many diverse diseases. He who brought the dead Lazarus back to life is now himself about to die. All that was once pleasing about him has now become a cause for sadness, and all that was sweetness in him has now turned into bitterness.

Though compassed by so many storms of evil, this shining Star of the Sea keeps her thoughts permanently fixed on

God and will not allow herself to be overcome by man's iniquity. Therefore, she stands next to the Cross, maintaining
her constancy, exhibiting her patience, manifesting her loyalty, proving her love—fearless of those who threaten her
with death and ignoring those who shower her with curses.
She endures all this with equal calm and by remaining silent
before her abusive enemies, she imitates her humble Son.

No discourteous words fall from her lips, nor does she
show any indignation in her gestures. She only utters deep
sighs, weeps profusely, suffers profoundly, and intimately shares
in her Son's pain. Her affliction is beyond words! She expresses no anger against those crucifying her Son, but prays
for them—evil though they be. She feels a sadness in her
heart for those ridiculing Christ and she grieves for those
who blaspheme him. Thus, with tears flowing down her face,
the Mother of Jesus stands at the foot of the Cross, and by
this example of her loving patience, she is a model to all
who are troubled by trials and tribulation.

All of you, who pass Mount Calvary, gaze upon holy Mary
as she stands there full of sorrow. Look to the right of the
Cross and there you will see Mary, the Mother of Christ—
has there ever been any sorrow like unto her sorrow, or has
there ever been in this world a Mother who suffered so lovingly with her Son as she? For every lesion that Jesus received in his body, she suffered a wound in her soul, and
whenever she saw those wounds bleed, she underwent a
martyrdom.

Devout soul, see to it that you treasure all these things in
the depths of your breast. When the time of tribulation comes
upon you, be meek as well as courageous. And when something you especially love is taken from you, or when something you deem necessary is denied you, neither be disturbed
nor yield to despair. For Jesus' dearest friends are often tried
by such severe struggles. If God did not spare his own Son,

but delivered him up to such unspeakable suffering for our benefit, why are you hankering for the joys of this world?

If Christ did not seek himself but was obedient and ready to endure all that was most painful and vile, why do you fear what is trying and toilsome, when for the love of the Crucified you should embrace whatever is difficult and demanding? If he permitted his most holy Mother to endure much adversity during her life and allowed her to face much distress, to suffer intensely and to weep copious tears, how then can you live in this world without some anxiety? If you consider all of God's friends, you will find that there is none who sailed through life without being tested to some degree. Look upon the Crucified and his Blessed Mother as an example of persevering patience, and do not be afraid to sustain some small inconvenience in return for Jesus' infinite love, so that when his glory will be revealed, as he has promised, you will have the endless joy of seeing God face to face.

The most lovable Mother of Jesus knew what it was to suffer in union with those struggling under affliction, for from her own experience she learned to extend love and compassion to the unfortunate. Nor will she forget her own poor; she will attend to their prayers; at the proper time she will assist those who invoke her aid; and she will show herself favorable to all who honor her.

Most merciful Jesus, loving Son of Mary, grant me the grace of holy tears; pierce and fill my heart with the same burning compassion that I know filled your Mother's heart! Look upon me with the same eyes of love as you looked upon your Mother and your beloved disciple—both standing in tears at the foot of your Cross—at the moment when you commended one to the other and bade them your final farewell with these most affectionate of words: *Behold your son, behold your mother!* I ask you to visit me, before I should die, with your gift of salvation, and let me hear those very same words that Blessed John heard from the Cross: *Behold your mother!* On hearing these my soul will then feel perfectly safe and will no longer have any fear of the enemy, who roams about seeking my ruin.

O Holy Mary, my most gentle Lady, faithful Advocate of all Christians, in view of the extraordinary merits that were yours and which made you most pleasing to God, and in view of your every comforting gesture you made to your Son, as well as the countless tears you shed during his most bitter Passion, I ask you to have pity on me, poor creature that I am. Take me under your maternal care and include me among the number of your servants, whom you hold dear and embrace with your special love.

O glorious Virgin Mary, my only hope, before my soul should leave this body of mine, come and reveal your face to me. Direct your gentle and beautiful eyes of mercy toward me, the very eyes that had joyfully and so often looked upon the fruit of your womb, Jesus, and were wetted because of the many tears shed during his Passion. Most holy Mother of Jesus, come and stand at my side together with your group of attending virgins and the holy assemblage of saints, as you had steadfastly and perseveringly stood unto the end, when your most beloved Son was about to die on the Cross. After my Lord Jesus Christ, your only Son, I find none so generous and eager to console someone in need as you, most amiable Mother of the Afflicted.

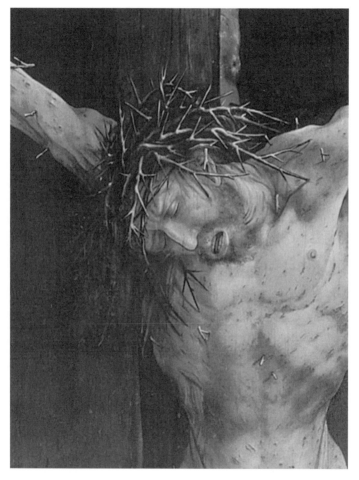

Crucifixion

Chapter 27

The lone dereliction of the Lord Jesus on his Cross

LORD JESUS CHRIST, beloved Son of the Father's special love, I bless and thank you for your overpowering lone dereliction on the Cross. In your most difficult hour you were abandoned by God the Father, by the entire heavenly host, and by all creatures of this earth. You felt as if you were a stranger or someone unknown, as if you were not the true Son of God, but one who was powerless and worthless. Only your sorrowful Mother, together with the disciple to whom you commended her and a few feeble women, remained at your side, and she could hardly speak a single word to you because of her grief and anxiety.

I praise and glorify you for your powerful outburst, when in the presence of so many bystanders, you shouted that tragic lament: *Eloi, Eloi, lama sabachthani.*[1] These words distinctly disclosed the depth of your affliction, your loss of all consolation, and the degree of your suffering to achieve the salvation of mankind. Mankind, in turn, looked upon you as a nothing, in fact, you were considered as the worst of criminals and, therefore, as one totally unworthy of life.

[1] Mark 15:34.

My soul, pay special attention to these words of Jesus for they were primarily spoken for your instruction. This is the wonder of it all: the Lord of all things, who has need of nothing, has been brought to such a measure of misery as to speak his needs into his Father's ears. He, who cooperates in all that the Father does, now complains that the Father has abandoned him; he, who sustains all things without difficulty, now reveals that he is heavily weighted down; he who was accustomed to console the sorrowful and the sickly now confesses that he is helpless and a stranger; he who was appointed to receive everyone's prayer and habitually hears the cry of the poor now voices his humble appeal: *My God, my God, why have you forsaken me?*[2] From the very beginning of his Passion until now, never has Christ uttered so lamentable a cry!

I, therefore, acknowledge your lament, O Christ, which, in your passible flesh, you spoke for my benefit from the Cross. Your abandonment becomes my consolation, your complaint my encouragement, your weakness my strength, and your chastisement is the satisfaction paid for all my sins and transgressions.

You are the heavenly Physician, who, out of immense love and compassion, freely took upon yourself this suffering and punishment. You, thus, chose to become weak with those who are weak, sorrowful with those in sorrow, sad with those in sin. In addition you befriended those under oppression and pleaded for all your weak members. These words of yours, therefore, were not born of despair or defiance, but flowed from your sensitive human nature. Indeed, your flesh, which knew not sin's stain, endured its penalty, and your innocent body underwent the most painful punishment, while your

[2] Mark 15:34.

soul enjoyed supreme beatitude. Your being divine in no way lessened your suffering, rather your divinity became manifest in your remarkable strength and forbearance, while accomplishing the redemption of the human race.

Who is the faithful soul, who will not feel compassion on hearing these words? Who is so callous as not to be pricked by this cry, this utterance? Even the unfeeling elements burst forth with stupendous signs of their sympathy. From the sixth to the ninth hour, the sun withdrew its luminous rays from the earth, so unwilling was it to shine on those unworthy. And the earth itself quaked and quivered at the injuries done to its Creator and lamented that the Author of life should suffer such punishment. The elements thus made it known that they did not want to see him die.

Since you are endowed with reason, you should join in their mourning, while the sun grieves and the earth trembles. Attend to Jesus' words; understand why he cries out and what that cry means. Throughout his anguish and affliction, the Lord Jesus remained calm and patient—nothing but sweetness and affection escaped his lips. He directs his prayer to the Father above and mentions no other name than that of God, and this only to bring his desolation to his notice. He asks no comfort from his Mother and from his friends he asks no assistance.

Jesus is thus instructing you as to how you should imitate him, when you yourself feel desolate. If you are infirm in body, or if you find that you are mentally weary and depressed, or if others despise you, or you lose the good graces of men because of your poverty or some inadequacy, do not give in to sadness or yield to anger. Rather, let this be your way of acting: choose this scene as your safe refuge and enter into conversation with Jesus, despised and hanging on his Cross and abandoned for a time by the Father, and reflect on what he meant when he uttered the words: *My God, my God, why have you forsaken me?*

When you are ill, be sure to be gentle and kind, and do not chafe if those serving you sometimes neglect you, or if the brethren rarely visit you. Think of Jesus, forsaken on his Cross, and stop complaining about trifling inconveniences. Ask Jesus to come to you and seek your support in him, for he can change your desolation into consolation. Forget about this world's disappointing comforts and do not fret about whether your friends love you; rather desire that the angels always be your companions and ask the saints to pray for you. Lift up your eyes to the Crucified and meditate on his sacred wounds. Implore the glorious Virgin by pouring out a special prayer in her honor, for she alone stood staunchly at the foot of the Cross and heard Jesus crying out in a loud voice to the Father. Clear your head of all worldly thoughts and images and concentrate on your heavenly homeland. Cherish God as your Father, Jesus as your brother, Mary as your mother, the angels as your friends, and the saints as your relatives. For you are descended from a noble and distinguished family—not according to the flesh but in the freedom of the Spirit. Surrounded by such spiritual defenses and with so many dear patrons upon whom you can call for assistance, you can confidently await the day of the final Judgment and anchor your hope in the goodness of the merciful Savior.

Supreme and revered Father of my Lord Jesus Christ, I beseech you to look kindly on the prayer of your servant, which he humbly offers to you today, through the hands of your beloved Son, as he hangs on the Cross. Pardon all the sins I have committed, and do not for any length of time keep the gift of heaven's grace from me or allow me to be endangered by severe temptations or harassed by disquieting passions.

Prove me, Lord, and test me, for you know what is best for me. Preserve my soul and during time of temptation also provide me with the strength to overcome them. Take what the scheming enemy has contrived for my soul's detriment and turn it into a means for gaining salvation and for a greater increase of your grace. Be my bulwark and be ever near me, especially when I am heavily weighted down with trials and have very little trust in other human beings. In such times of critical need, you remain my faithful friend. If I am to be tested and to be deprived of your consolation for a time, then grant me to bear it patiently and to commit my entire burden trustingly into your care, and also grant that I may call to mind the hour of desolation that your most beloved and favored Son, Jesus, experienced, when in his most trying moment and when he was without friends, you alone were in his thoughts.

Chapter 28

On the thirst of the Lord Jesus
as he hangs on the Cross

LORD JESUS CHRIST, Fountain of living water and Source of salvific wisdom, I bless and thank you for the acute thirst you experienced as you hung on your Cross. Inasmuch as your sacred and precious blood had flowed from you and all your body's natural liquids were consumed—this was due to the excessive torture that you endured—your body was completely dry and so you thirsted. You thirsted still more, however, because of your ardent desire for our salvation, and very much like a poor beggar you asked for a drink saying: *I thirst.*[1] But to this simple request there was no one who would respond, not even to offer a cup of cool water to you, who made all the waters of this world.

There were those standing nearby who heard this request, but rather than being moved to pity they were incited to greater brutality. Satisfying the malice they nourished in their breasts, they soaked a sponge in vinegar mixed with gall and offered this most bitter draft to your sweet lips. Such a drink would not even have been given to dogs.

I praise and honor you, for your humble resignation in accepting and tasting that acerbic drink; you did this to expiate the illicit delights that our first parents experienced. As

[1] John 19:28.

the tasting of that forbidden fruit brought death into the world, so your tasting of that bitter draft becomes medicine for our salvation.

But woe to you, an unbelieving people, a stiff-necked and degenerate race! How could you have so turned around as to free Barabbas and to crucify Christ? How could you have fallen into such insanity as to offer vinegar, when a refreshing drink was requested? Try offering such a drink to your high priest or to one of the rulers of the people and see if they would agree to drink it! What did Christ do to you, or in which way did Jesus of Nazareth antagonize you? Answer me, I beseech you!

Did not God send down manna from heaven for you, and did he not bring forth water from a huge boulder, so that you might eat and drink your fill? And now, in return for the sweet tasting manna you offer him wine mixed with myrrh, and in return for the abundant waters that freely flowed forth you offer the thirsty Christ not even a single drop.

If Christ so desired, he could have turned all your waters into salt water, and when both bread and water were lacking, you would perish because of extreme interior dryness, and all this because you refused to show pity. In fact, if Christ had actually desired a refreshing drink, the holy angels would certainly have quickly and willingly brought him a lifesaving liquor from heaven—sweeter than any known—as they had, on another occasion, brought him food after he was thrice tempted by the devil in the desert. But Christ was unwilling to vindicate himself and he did not choose to manifest his power by a miracle. Rather, he chose to show his patience and longsuffering, so that he could give an example to all who have professed vows of poverty.

And you, who are a disciple of Jesus, drink from this cup with its bitter contents as a remedy against a gluttonous appetite. If you wish to share Christ's banquet in the kingdom of his Father, then do not let your heart crave sumptuous dishes or expensive wines, neither comfortable couches nor fine clothing. Such things are altogether contrary to Jesus' simple manner of life and sorrowful Passion.

Do not permit yourself to be overcome by the delights of the flesh, but keep a rein on the stirrings of concupiscence by exercising moderation at table. However, if you have gone overboard by overeating or in your desire for delicacies, then set this aright by daily labors and night vigils, at the same time reflecting with sadness on the bitter cup that Christ was given to drink.

O Jesus, heavenly manna and sweet nectar, as you hung upon your Cross you experienced an uncommon thirst, but you were not offered the least bit of water to refresh you, instead you were given vinegar and gall to drink. When I sit down for a meal let me remember this bitter draft of yours, so that I may not be overly concerned about my body's nourishment but may be entirely absorbed with the sacred reading.

May I learn to take only as much food as is necessary and to return sincere thanks to you for benefits received. Let me not grumble about the quantity or quality of the food served, otherwise I should consider myself unworthy to be fed by the alms received from the poor and ashamed to be supported by another's hard labor. Lord, grant that I may hunger for the food that does not perish but remains unto eternal life. Also grant that I may thirst for the fountain of everlasting life and that I may now and then pick up from the heavenly banquet table a crumb of the living bread and taste its true flavor, even though it be of short duration, and experientially taste how sweet is your spirit that you pour into the hearts of your children of grace.

Chapter 29

On fulfilling the Scriptures in the death of Christ and on the words *It is finished!*

LORD JESUS CHRIST, Revealer of deep mysteries and Fulfiller of the law and the prophets, I bless and thank you for having perfectly accomplished your Father's will as expressed in those few appropriate words, which you fittingly pronounced immediately after receiving the vinegar: *It is finished!*[1] These words sum up your entire life. It is as if you were saying: "Now is fulfilled all that the Old Law had foretold of me, and all that the sacred ceremonies and sacrificial rites of former years had prefigured. The predictions of the holy prophets are finally realized as well as the long hoped for desires of the ancient patriarchs. All that pertains to the redemption of the human race has been wonderfully brought about, and all the promises found in the heaven given Sacred Scriptures have all been clearly fulfilled as regards to time and place, and everything has now come to a happy end. The few things that remain will undoubtedly come to pass in due time. I have obeyed my Father's commands; he had sent me into the world and I have completed the work he had entrusted to me.

[1] John 19:30.

"In my time I have cured the sick, have given clear proof of my divinity, and as the Father has taught me, so I preached to the world, never keeping any saving doctrine from the ears of the faithful. For thirty-three years I have walked this earth as a pilgrim, enjoyed my dealings with men and frequently have become tired from my journeying. I was cruelly calumniated by my adversaries, betrayed by a disciple, abandoned by friends, taken captive by enemies, scourged by their servants, condemned by judges, mocked by chief priests, and here I now hang on a Cross, innocent though I be.

"What more should I have done that I have not done? What more should I have suffered and have not suffered? If I have done or endured less than I should have, then I am ready to make up for it before I die. In fact, my death will pay every debt in full. Today I have finished all that I had to do. I will not allow my death to be postponed; it is out of pure love that I freely lay down my life for my sheep. At this hour, when I know that the first man had incurred perpetual death by eating of the forbidden tree, I willingly accept the death of my body for the transgressions of sinners—though in no way have I merited this death.

"All that pertains to me will soon come to an end. I will not speak many more words in this world, because I will not be here much longer, for I hasten to the Father. All labors will cease, sorrow and grief will vanish, conflicts will be no more, troubles will be unknown, and by my death, death itself will be overcome.

"There remains nothing more to be done, except to commend my spirit to my Father and to leave my body behind until the third day. This I certainly know, that men imbued with pity and mindful of former friendships will take that body with them and place it in a new tomb. Therefore, to indicate that all the requirements of the Old Law have been properly fulfilled, and to establish that of the

New, I hereby declare to all listening my final but brief remark: *It is finished.*"

O Lord Jesus Christ, illustrious and wise Master, it is indeed just as you state and affirm. There is nothing objectionable in your words. By your divine actions you have confirmed all that you say and you have shown how the oracles of the prophets had been fulfilled in you.

Now is the time for you to rest from all labor, to rest from all that you have done while you were on earth. In the beginning, Lord, you have created all things with the Father, and now in cooperation with the Father you have made all things new. In six days you made all that is in this world of ours, and in the sixth age of the world you completed the work of man's redemption. On the sixth day you formed man from the slime of the earth, and on the sixth day you redeemed him by your blood. Adam was tempted and deceived by Eve on the sixth day, and on the sixth day you were announced by an angel and were conceived in the Virgin's womb. On the sixth day man sinned and lost paradise, and on the sixth day you suffered for our sins and mercifully received the thief into paradise. In order that recent times should correspond to those of old, and that the deeds of today correspond to those of yesterday, it was fitting that your sixth utterance from the Cross be: *It is finished.*

Continue on your way, Lord Jesus, wherever you will; and now that you have accomplished your great work of mercy on earth, return to your Father in heaven. Precede your servants, prepare the way so that they may quickly follow you. Open the door to the heavenly kingdom, which our first parents' audacity had caused to be closed for so long a time. Go and visit the Holy Fathers in the abode of the dead, shed light on those sitting in darkness, destroy the power of the devil, loosen the chains of those bound, grant rest to those who are weary, console those who mourn, deliver those who await you, and liberate your captives from the lower regions. After you have led and placed them in the heavenly mansions with the angelic host, then, in your kingdom, remember me, Lord, and release me from this prison, from this abode of flesh and slime, from my ever-threatening surroundings, and finally from this deceitful and miserable world.

You, who profess to follow Christ, imitate him in fulfilling this utterance of his, and as long as you have the strength and the time, do not seek to end your labors. Complete what you have begun, so that when you come to the evening of life, you too can say with your friend Jesus: *It is finished.* Therefore, walk along the path of true virtue, pursue righteousness, resist sin even unto death, so that you may gain eternal life and be able to say with Saint Paul: *I have fought the good fight, I have finished the race, I have kept the faith.* [2] You still have some labors ahead of you and some time left on this earth. Your hour will come quickly, when *being made perfect in a short period of time, you fulfilled a long time.* [3]

O Jesus Christ, Lord of heaven and earth, outstanding and perfect Model of all virtues and everlasting Reward for good deeds, direct all my actions so that they may always please you, and enlighten and purify the thoughts in my mind. Teach me humbly to begin all my works for the praise and glory of your holy name, that I may diligently see them through, and bring them to a happy conclusion. Grant that I not become negligent before the time appointed by the Father, but that I may work for the reward of eternal life day and night in the vineyard of holy religion, and wholeheartedly exert myself in the school of godly exercises until my soul leaves me.

[2] 2 Timothy 4:7.
[3] See Wisdom 4:13.

Finally, I ask that in my final hour and after much toil and labor, I may, with happiness of heart, say with you: *It is finished.*

Good Jesus, grant me reward for my labors, repose for my fatigue, joy for my sorrows, a crown for my struggles, glory for my humiliations, and beatitude for the miseries I endured living in this world. In this place of pilgrimage, you were and are the final cause of all my actions. Be now my reward in the kingdom of heaven, because I desire to have you alone as the recompense of my labors, you, who are the beatitude and glory of all your saints.

Chapter 30

On the Lord Jesus' sorrowful
departure from this world

LORD JESUS CHRIST, Life of the living, Hope of the dying, Salvation of all who hope in you, I bless and thank you for your temporary departure from this world, and for your joyful return to the Father through the terrible throes of death and the marvelous martyrdom of the Cross.

I praise and glorify you for the pallid expression on your face at the approach of death, your final last-minute agony, your total loss of bodily strength, and the bitter breaking of your love-filled heart, when you, who endow all spirits with life, did not cringe when it was time for you to submit to death, so that you could open for us the way to the kingdom of heaven.

I praise and glorify you for the strong and loud cry you gave forth from the cross, a cry that exceeded the powers of any ordinary human being. I praise you for the sad and sorrowful separation of your noble soul from your beloved body, for the holy commendation of your spirit into your Father's hands, for the humble lowering of your sacred and thorn-crowned head on your revered breast—a sign of your ever-faithful filial obedience, for your generous giving of your most holy soul for the world's salvation, and for the final utterance of your mortal life, when you broke forth with these words in pious prayer: *Father, into your hands I commend*

my spirit.[1] Immediately after you said this, you yielded up
your spirit and, thus, you completed your earthly pilgrimage
and fell into a serene sleep.

O how precious and victorious was that death, which destroyed our death and gave us eternal life! O Christ, may
your death be ever fixed in my memory so that whenever I
think of your death I may also be mindful of my own, and
when the uncertain time for my life's end does come, I may
not be overcome by fear or despair.

This is the hour of which you were aware from the first
moment of your conception, and toward which you hastened as a traveler does toward his homeland or a wise
workman hastens to accomplish his task. You left the high-
est of the heavens to come into our world, and from this
world you descended into the abode of the dead, and from
there you retraced your way to your throne in the high
heavens.

My soul, deep anguish should be yours because of the bitter
death suffered by your beloved Lord and God. Reflect on the
manner of Jesus' death and on the signs that accompanied his
death. Notice how the Just One dies and no one takes it to heart;
no one realizes who or how wonderful he is, except his poor
sorrowing Mother, who, with several of her friends, stands
weeping at the foot of the Cross. She sees her loving Son hanging before her, his body naked and covered with blood; she sees
his body gradually lose its color; she sees him in agony and hears
his dying cry. After witnessing all this, no wonder she grieves
pitifully and grows pale; her soul swoons seeing her crucified
and dead Savior before her.

Go, stand beside Mary next to the Cross, and with sadness
of heart meditate on Jesus' death. Observe how Jesus, who is

[1] Luke 23:46.

innocent, dies naked and like an outcast. Never was there a man more wretched than he! There was never anyone more beloved by God, nor anyone more despised by men than Jesus of Nazareth, who was crucified by his own people.

Notice the gratitude that the world shows him in return for all of his extraordinary deeds and miracles. He is put to death as if he were the worst of thieves and dies as the poorest of men. He does not die in a comfortable feather bed, but on the hard wood of the Cross; not in a house or under a protecting roof, but in the open air, in a frightfully foul place; not in a private room, but publicly on a Cross; not in the company of his disciples, but between two thieves; not in the arms of his loving Mother, but between those of a tall Cross.

He did not even have a few handfuls of straw beneath him, nor over him a covering of the poorest linen. He had no pillow for his head, but a crown of sharp thorns instead. There were no sandals on his feet nor gloves on his hands, but as substitutes he had iron nails that pierced through his flesh and bones.

In this dire distress of his, there was no one to minister to him, but an impenitent thief at his side, a degenerate criminal, who showered him with shameful insults. There was no one to console him—his followers and those with whom he had frequently sat at table had all but deserted him. He could move neither hand nor foot, nor turn on his side—he found no relief for his body's pain, not even in the slightest. He remained immobile, stretched to the straining point, every organ dreadfully distended. No one there tried to console him. No one thought of helping him. No one was interested in him. His heart all but stopped beating.

There remained only his tongue that he could use. He prayed for his enemies, and from the pulpit of the Cross he preached seven worthy words counter to the seven deadly sins. Nor was his tongue without its torment, for when he was thirsty it was given vinegar and gall. From the soles of his feet to the crown of his head he was bathed in the waters of suffering, and finally at about the ninth hour he gave a loud cry and died.

Who is this who cries out with his final breath? How distinguished he must be at whose passing both heaven and earth mourn, from whose sight death flees, at whose voice the dead rise, at whose visage the gates of death are shattered, whose presence the devil cannot endure, whose power no one can resist, before whom hell trembles and heaven worships, whom the angels serve and the archangels obey, by whose splendor the limbo of the fathers is aglow, the assembly of saints rejoices, their fetters are removed and the many captive souls are brought into the light.

The centurion who was standing there remarked: *Truly, he was the Son of God.*[2] That blessed man, upon seeing that Jesus gave up his spirit after he had cried out, discerned the hidden divinity within that human nature and immediately acknowledged that he, whom his own people had despised and crucified, was the Son of God.

O you hard-hearted people, you are neither appeased by the victim's sufferings, nor are you persuaded by the unusual prodigies at his death. You, who once asked for signs from heaven, are deaf and blind. But now you must see and listen. Signs certainly appeared in the heavens above and on the earth below. The elements of this earth are Christ's servants, and at the hour of his demise they all went into mourning, while you wretches laughed. The sun went dark at noon, so as not to witness his death, and the earth quaked fearfully, because it could not calmly tolerate the injury done to God. Rocks were torn asunder and with loud voices they mourned

[2] Mark 15:39.

their Creator. The veil of the temple was torn in two—this rending indicated that Christ's sacred mysteries are now made manifest to all.

Christ himself is the true Victim, who takes away all the sins of the world. He is the immaculate Lamb of God, sacrificed on the Cross during the Paschal season. He is the true Priest consecrated by God, and as such has offered himself up as a Victim to the Father in an odor of sweetness. He is the High Priest who once a year enters alone into the Holy of Holies to plead not only for his own people, but for the salvation of all peoples who believe in him. And this Christ truly did, dying once for the entire human race until the end of time.

Tombs were also opened to show that the coming Resurrection of Christ and of the saints was near. And many who had come to witness this scene understood these prodigies and, with consciences powerfully touched, they returned home beating their breasts.

And you, my soul, enter into your most inner self and mourn with those who mourn and weep with those who weep for Christ, lest you be found to be harder than a rock and more faithless than that crowd of observers. Blessed are the tears shed out of love for the Crucified, for it is both holy and fitting to weep for the loving Lord. To weep copious tears out of compassion for one's beloved is in itself a great consolation to that lover's soul. Jesus himself often wept over man's miseries, and when he had no more tears to shed, he shed his blood with even greater love.

The Lord Jesus Christ died for you on the Cross, therefore, let this world be altogether dead to you. From Jesus' death learn to be mindful of your own and strive to prepare yourself for it. You do not know when the Lord will come, nor do you know when your Maker will call you from this world. So, every hour be on your watch, and pray that you will find your final hour a pleasant hour.

Speak and act as if you are to depart this very day. Learn to die before you actually die, so that when death does come it will not be a horror to you but the gateway to life. Christ has died and so have the prophets, and you too will soon have to follow the way of your fathers. But there is great hope and great consolation in these words of Jesus: *Whoever believes in me, even if he should die, will live,*[3] and again, *Whoever hears my word and believes in him who sent me, will have eternal life.*[4] Therefore, while you are still alive, have Jesus as your friend, so that when you do die, you will find him favorable to you.

Throw aside whatever keeps you from the love of Jesus and whatever makes it difficult for you to enter the kingdom of heaven. Beware of anything that can sully the purity of your conscience and leave behind all that can rob you of your peace of mind. Cut yourself off from the world, but remain united to God and be a close companion of Christ. Walk with Jesus in the freedom of the spirit and do not concern yourself with this world's affairs. Prepare your heart to receive him and show him a large furnished chamber, so that he and his disciples can celebrate the mystical Pasch with you before you die.

When you find your health beginning to give way, and you feel that the time for you to be called hence is near at hand, then offer this humble prayer to Jesus, using the words of Mary and Martha: *Lord, the one you love is sick.*[5] The mighty and merciful Jesus, who wept for Lazarus and raised him from the dead, can also heal your wounds and raise your dead body up on the last day. Give special thought to the Lord's Supper, when Jesus humbly washed the feet of his disciples and before leaving them he instituted for their spiritual comfort the Sacrament of his

[3] John 11:26.
[4] John 5:24.
[5] John 11:3.

sacred Body. Then meekly ask the Lord Jesus to absolve you from all your loathsome sins and generously to strengthen you, before you depart on our journey, by receiving his precious Body. After you have received this, make your thanksgiving and meditate devoutly on the consoling words of his new commandment and then, with eyes raised to heaven, desire from the depths of your heart to be united to Christ. Following this, turn your thoughts to Christ's Passion and draw true consolation from that source. Enter with Jesus and his disciples into the garden near the Mount of Olives and, though your friends are present, retire within yourself so that you may more freely and privately spend time with God, praying to your heavenly Father for a happy ending to your earthly sojourn. Kneel next to Jesus and, falling forward on your face on the earth, abandon yourself into God's hands and speak these most perfect words of Christ: *Father, not my will, but your will be done.*[6] He knows better than anyone whether living or dying is more advantageous for your soul's salvation.

Ask your brethren and all your devoted friends who come to see you, to watch with you in prayer, lest the devil attempt to disturb you with his deceits. When anxiety takes hold of you, turn to Jesus and follow him as he carries his Cross to Mount Calvary. Make that your final station; choose to have your life end there, and there hand over your spirit. Place Jesus' Passion and death between you and your future judgment and with steadfast gaze look upon the Crucified. If the devil tries to terrorize you, invoke the name of Jesus and raise the standard of the holy Cross. If he counters by narrating your many sins and past misdeeds, then respond by reciting the infinite merits of Christ.

Also remember the seven words Jesus spoke from the Cross for your instruction. As soon as he and his Cross were raised

[6] See Luke 22:42.

on high, he prayed for his enemies and forgave them their sins. This he did so that you too might, from the depths of your heart, forgive all who have wronged you, and once again you should ask that your sins be forgiven.

Second, he promised the penitent thief the joys of paradise, and this that you might not yield to despair because of the enormity of your sins, but that you might confidently ask him to be remembered in the kingdom of heaven.

Third, he commended his Blessed Mother, the Virgin, to the virgin John, so that when you are in your final agony, you may trustingly turn to Mary, his most loving Mother, Help of Christians, and that you may also confidently commend yourself to the blessed apostle John and all the saints. Commend yourself likewise to the prayers of your brethren and devoted friends, that after your death they may be kind enough to remember you in their prayers and Masses.

Fourth, Jesus revealed that he felt abandoned in his sufferings. Do not give in to impatience when you feel yourself overburdened with many worries. If you are not relieved of them in time, then submit to the divine will as in all things.

Fifth, Jesus said: *I thirst*, so that you may eagerly thirst after God, the living fountain, and desire to die and to be with him. This is far better than prolonging one's pilgrimage in this world and exposing oneself to its constant dangers.

Sixth, he spoke: *It is finished*, so that when you sense that your final days are near, you are to praise God for all the good you have accomplished in your life—and ask that whatever you have done less than well—be wholly remedied by Christ.

Seventh, with a loud cry he placed his soul into his Father's hands to teach you that, when you are about to depart this world, you are not to be remiss in voicing and frequently repeating the words of his final commendation. You will find at the end that there are none more meaningful than these.

O most loving Jesus, Splendor of the Father's glory and Sun of righteousness, you have chosen to suffer so shameful a punishment for me your unworthy servant, and on Mount Calvary you delivered your soul to the Father for the world's redemption and commended it to him with a prayer. Grant that I may always carry in my heart a sorrow and a love for your most dolorous death. Also grant that by mortifying all my sinful inclinations I may daily share in your death, and that when my end approaches I may be found worthy to dwell in the light of your mercies and joyfully enter with you into paradise.

Be with me, Lord, as I lie dying, strengthen me in my agony, visit me when I call upon you, defend me from my enemies, free me from my anxieties, console me in my mourning, be my comfort when I am fearful, revive me when I feel faint, and finally, receive me when I die.

May your last word from the Cross be also my final word in this life. And when I am no longer able to utter another word, let this express my definitive desire: "Father, into your hands I commend my spirit. O Lord, God of Truth, you have redeemed me. Amen."

Chapter 31

On the pitiable appearance of Jesus after his soul left his body

LORD JESUS CHRIST, spotless Mirror of the Divine Majesty, I bless and thank you for your pallid and pitiable appearance at the onset of death, for as soon as your soul left your body clear signs of mortality set in. Alas, Jesus, the handsomest of men, your appealing and comely countenance was stained by the sordid spitting of unclean lips, and in your combat with death the glow of your gracious youth deserted you.

All this befell you, O most loving God, because of your desire to cleanse me of my sins. You allowed your body to be disfigured so that my soul might be purified, and you experienced a most horrible death so that I might be delivered from eternal death.

Death, what have you done? Were you not afraid to lay your hands on the Lord's anointed? What rights do you have over him, or what defects have you discovered in the Son of God? You have attacked and assassinated him, but not without doing injury to yourself. By destroying life, you destroyed yourself, and because you have been pierced by the talons of Christ's Divinity, you have lost your authority over your fiendish domain. By Christ's descent into the abode of the dead, you were forced to surrender all the elect who had died in Adam's sin, and who, for so long a time, had been held captive by the prince of darkness. It was thus foretold by the prophet: *Death, I shall be your death; hell, I shall be your sting.*[1] And appropriately it is resonantly sung in the Church: *Life dies upon the tree, the grave is deprived of its sting.*[2]

Therefore, O Christ, by your dying the promise of life was restored to me, and with your conquering of the prince of death, a crown of joy was given me. In fact, when you succumbed on the wood of the Cross, many magnificent graces flowed from you and these have enriched our lives. The fruits derived from your Passion are inexhaustible: original sin is obliterated, personal sins are pardoned, forgiveness is more easily obtained, punishment is lessened, vengeance is suspended, all debts are paid, and mercy is shown to all who are contrite.

Lord, you did not die in vain. But for whom, then, did you die? Certainly, not for the angels, for they always remained steadfast in the truth. As for the devils, after their fall from heaven their wills became more and more obdurate, and as a result they could not be reinstated. Therefore, it was for man that you died. Deceived by the devil's wiles, man fell and became liable to death, and so it was fitting that he, whom another's malice had brought to ruin, should be raised up by another's love.

O how great is that love of God and how unfathomable his wisdom! This is the astounding and ever-memorable mystery: it is through the Cross that man is saved; it is through disgrace that man enters the kingdom; it is through suffering that he achieves glory; and it is through death that he attains eternal life.

Your holy Passion, Lord, is the medicine for all our wounds. Your Cross is the defeat of all our enemies and the unfailing defense of all who believe in you. Your death is the term of our vices and the source of our virtues.

---

[1] Hosea 13:14.

[2] From the Responsory at the end of Tenebrae, as in use during the Middle Ages. See W. Duthoit's translation of Thomas à Kempis' *Prayers and Meditations on the Life of Christ* (London: Kegan Paul, French, Trübner, 1908), p. 177.

Thus, I rejoice in the benefits and fruits flowing from your Passion. I find consolation in the fact that you have redeemed me, but because of my love for you, I am at the same time saddened by your most painful death. It is a holy thing to rejoice with you because you conquered death, and it is also holy to condole with you because you endured such terrible suffering for me.

And now, faithful soul, look upon the sad and sallow face of your crucified Savior. Look intently on the various members of his dead body, and from your deep-seated compassion let the tears flow freely from your eyes. By gazing upon Jesus hanging on his Cross, you will spend your time most worthily, for your thoughts will then be given over to things holy and sublime. The image of the Crucified in the heart of the just man is like *a cluster of henna from the vineyards of Engedi.*[3]

If you are moved with pity and your heart abounds with humane sentiments, then raise your mind and heart to contemplate your God, who suffered crucifixion on your behalf and now hangs dead on the Cross. *Behold the wood of the Cross, on which your salvation hangs.*[4] The Cross is the redemption of the believer but to the unbeliever an object of scorn.

Christ's thorn-crowned head lies low on his sacred breast, and no longer are there any signs of life in him. His eyes see nothing—and yet nothing is secret or hidden from him. His ears hear nothing—and yet he knows all things even before they come to pass. He, who endows all flowers with sweet scents, smells nothing, and he, who gives life and supplies food to all the living, has lost his taste. He, who opened the mouths of the dumb, is now unable to move his lips, and he, who taught his followers, cannot utter a single word. The

---

[3] Song of Songs 1:14; henna is a plant that bears white scented flowers.

[4] This is a slight variation of the antiphon sung during the unveiling of the Cross during the Good Friday service.

tongue that spoke only the truth is now silenced, and the face once brighter than the sun is now without color.

His cheeks, fair as those of a turtledove, have lost their radiance, and his hands, that stretched out the heavens above, are pierced by hard and sharp nails. His knees, so accustomed to being bent in prayer, are now naked and limp, and his legs, those marble columns[5] that used to support his body's weight, are now unsteady and powerless. His feet, so often weary from going about preaching, are now iron-bound to the wood of the Cross.

Every part of his body has the appearance of excruciating pain. His body is fraught with wounds, and these are begrimed with blood. His bones were not broken as in the case of the two thieves, and this was so that the Sacred Scriptures might be fulfilled. He is the true Lamb, prefigured in the Old Law, whose bones are to remain intact.

Such is my beloved, O daughters of Jerusalem, such is my friend,[6] and it is to this deplorable condition that death has brought him. If I were to die a thousand times for him, it would still not be adequate compensation for his love.

O sweet Jesus, Redeemer of my soul, who can grant me to die with you on the Cross, and when it is time for me to leave my body to share in the happiness of that hour? I ask you from the bottom of my heart to allow me, in this frail body of mine, to live so as to direct all my actions and desires in accordance with your good pleasure, and that, after I prove myself through many a temptation, I may complete the course of my life in the state of grace and arrive at the reward of eternal beatitude.

---

[5] See Song of Songs 5:15. In enumerating the parts of the body, the author has the Song of Songs 5:10–16 in mind.

[6] Song of Songs 5:16.

Chapter 32

On the piercing of the sacred side
of the Lord Jesus after his death

LORD JESUS CHRIST, inexhaustible Fountain of love and grace, I bless and thank you for the ruthless piercing of your sacred side after you died. It was then that you, holiest of all who are holy, were brutally struck on your right side by one of the soldiers holding a military lance. It pierced so deeply that it entered the most tender part of your heart and from that wide-open wound there flowed a life-giving fountain of blood and water. Would that the whole world had been sprinkled, it might then be saved!

O holy and bountiful stream of blood from the right side of Christ—sleeping in death on the Cross—and flowing forth for the redemption of the human race! O pure and gentle outpouring of blessed water from the Savior's inmost parts for the washing away of our sins!

In earlier days, Moses, the servant of the Lord, struck the rock in the desert and there came forth a superabundance of water—the people drank joyfully from that torrent, as well as their cattle, and all murmuring came to an end. This time Longinus, a sturdy soldier, picked up a lance and with a strong arm gave a mighty blow to the Rock, opening the side of Christ, from which there continually flowed blood and water. It is from this source that our undefiled Mother, the Church, has drawn the sacraments of salvation. Just as Eve is called the mother of all the living and was formed from her husband Adam's rib, so the holy Church Militant is known as the mother of all the faithful, for she was formed from the side of Christ, her Spouse.

O noble and precious wound of my Lord, held in greater reverence than all his other wounds—so deeply pierced and widely opened that all the faithful might enter—miraculous in its flow, abundantly blessed, the last inflicted but the most beloved of all.

Whoever drinks from this most holy and sacred wound, or takes but one sip of love from it, will dismiss all his troubles, will be cured of all his burning desires for things temporal and carnal, will be aflame with a love for things eternal, and will be filled with the sweetness of the Holy Spirit, who will become in him a fountain of living water springing up to life eternal.

Enter, my soul, enter into your crucified Lord's right side. Enter by that noble wound to Jesus' most loving heart, transpierced out of love, and in the cleft of that Rock seek rest from this world's storms. Proceed, O man, to his inmost, hidden, and secret heart—to the heart of God who opens its door to you. Enter, you blessed of God! Why do you hesitate, standing outside? Waiting for you within is the river of life, the way of salvation, and the heavenly vault, whence spicy fragrances flow in abundance. Within is a haven, far from the gaze of your enemy and his temptations, and a place of loving mercy that preserves you from the wrath of future judgment.

Within is the ever-flowing fountain of oil and grace, which never ceases to extend mercy to sinners who approach with truly contrite hearts. Within is the source of the sacred river that flows from the center of paradise and waters the face of the earth, assuages the longings of thirsty souls, washes away sins, extinguishes impure inclinations, and subdues feelings of anger.

Therefore, drink a cup of the Savior's love from this fountain and from Jesus' side draw forth sweet consolation that you may no longer live in yourself but in him, who was wounded for you. Give your heart to him, who opened his heart to you.

Enter the opening of that sacred wound and pass to the Redeemer's innermost being. He invites you to enter; he asks you to abide with him; he desires that you and he have but one heart. He says: "Son, give me your heart." God asks nothing else of you. If you do give it, then you offer him the most acceptable of gifts. Give your heart to Jesus and to none other. Give it to Christ and not to the world. Give your heart to Eternal Wisdom and not to barren philosophy.

The reason why Christ had his side opened so widely and pierced so deeply is to give you easy access to your beloved's heart, that you might penetrate the inner being of the Son of God and be joined to him in a true union of hearts, also that all your affections might be directed to him, that all your works be done with simplicity of heart and in his honor, that you seek to please him alone, and that you strive to cling to him with all your mind and strength.

Where can you rest with greater security, or dwell more safely, or sleep more comfortably than in the wounds of Jesus Christ, who was crucified for you? Where will you find greater wisdom and more helpful knowledge on how to live than in the heart of Christ, who suffered for you, and from whose breast there flows a fountain of living water? When your love becomes lukewarm, where can it be instantly rekindled, or where can you be protected from this world's clamor, or become quickly recollected as in the heart of Jesus, pierced by a lance out of love for you?

There is nothing that so enflames, draws, and penetrates the heart of man as does the love of the crucified Redeemer. A certain saint[1] said: "My love has been crucified." To him I affectionately reply: "My love was wounded and pierced so that I might have easy access to his loving heart."

Then hasten, as much as holy desires urge you, and place your hand in Jesus' sacred side so that you may be marked with his blood and water. And if it be possible, take your own heart from you and place it next to Jesus' heart, and let him be its guardian, ruler, and owner so that worldly interests cannot get hold of it and corrupt it.

Open your heart to him and with great trust abandon yourself to him; offer him your every desire and non-desire. Be of one heart and soul with God so that in accordance with his supreme good pleasure, you may in all things think and feel as one with him, now and forever. When you give your heart totally to Jesus for him to possess and dwell within it, you will enjoy great peace of soul for you will not be readily annoyed or excessively saddened.

O most devoted Jesus, you are the source of all our hearts' secrets and you dwell in the hearts of those who love you! O crucified Lord, you are the object of all contemplation! O Divine Treasury of all gifts and graces, Christ the King and Redeemer of the faithful, you permitted your sacred side to be pierced by the head of a lance. Open for me, I ask, the door of your mercy and permit me to enter through that wide opening in your side to the innermost recesses of your most lovable heart so that my heart may become powerfully inflamed and be united to you by the insoluble bond of charity. May I live in you and you in me and may we remain united forever.

[1] See Ignatius of Antioch's *Letter to the Romans*, 7.

Pierce my heart with the arrow of your love. Let your soldier's spear pass into my inmost being and penetrate to my heart's interior, so that by this salutary wounding my soul may enjoy perfect health, acknowledge none but you as its beloved, and need no consolation other than you. May my heart be open and accessible to you alone, a stranger to the world, isolated from the devil, and by the sign of the Cross may it be fortified on all sides against all temptations.

The Deposition

Chapter 33

On the taking down of the
Lord Jesus from the Cross

LORD JESUS CHRIST, Fortitude Divine, I bless and thank you for your humility in being taken down from the tall Cross, on which, until sunset, you hung for our salvation. As evening came on, you were ordered to be taken down in accordance with the prescriptions of the old law, since the approaching Paschal Feast was to be kept on that holy Sabbath.

I praise and glorify you for the dedicated and loving attention shown you by your closest friends. When Joseph of Arimathea and Nicodemus, a teacher of the law—both illustrious gentlemen—came with their house servants to the Cross they set up ladders; one servant climbed up on the right, another on the left, while still another busied himself freeing your feet. With great deference and devotion they withdrew from your sacred hands and feet three precious nails—worth far more than glimmering gold—and with the aid of hardy companions they reverently took hold of your most noble body and slowly and cautiously lowered it to the ground.

Blessed are you, men of mercy, for showing such compassion to the Lord, your God, in your desire to give him fitting burial. The loyalty you previously showed your Friend when he was alive, is expressed, now that he is dead, with even greater reverence. Indeed, you will receive special recompense from God in heaven, because you have demonstrated your loyalty to him while on earth. And since you have already prepared a place of burial for him on earth, he himself will undoubtedly prepare a more blessed dwelling place for you in heaven, as he had promised his disciples the night before he died.

Would that I, the least of all servants of God, had been present at the burial of my Lord, so that I could have offered him some service, no matter how slight. I certainly would willingly have held the ladder next to the Cross or handed up the instrument used to pull out the nails or given a helping hand to those holding the body.

How fortunate I would have considered myself if I had been standing so near to the Cross as to receive, as a remembrance of his Passion, one of the Lord's nails as it fell on my breast from above. And as often as I gazed upon it, I would have been immediately reduced to tears.

I praise and honor you for that enviable embrace with which your most sorrowful Mother received you in her hands and clasped you in her arms, when your faithful and compassionate friends devoutly handed you to her and placed you in her virgin lap.

O how many tears did then flow from her most pure eyes, and how warm were the droplets that lingered on her chaste cheeks and then fell from her motherly countenance upon your broken body! O how pure the lips with which your most chaste Mother kissed your immobile limbs, and how intently and sorrowfully did she look upon your sacred wounds! O with what loving arms did she hold and enclose the blessed fruit of her womb, whom she saw immolated on the altar of the Cross for the world's salvation! Who is there among the devout who can fathom the depth of her sorrow or tell of the profusion of tears that Jesus' holy Mother then shed?

Now, my soul, draw nearer and devoutly kiss Jesus' ruby-stained wounds. When he was hanging, nailed to his Cross, there was no way of your getting near to him because of the crushing crowds and the height of the cross, but now he is lying wounded and dead in his grieving Mother's lap.

No matter how great a sinner you may be, or how acutely the fear of eternal damnation horrifies you, draw near, because it was for you that the Lamb was slaughtered and for you that the Victim, who has taken away the sin of the world, has been offered. So merciful and compassionate is the Lord Jesus, and so holy and sweet is Mary his Mother, that no one who wholeheartedly requests pardon goes away empty-handed or disappointed.

How heartwarming are these words to me, a sinner; they are sweeter to my heart than honey and the honeycomb. I well realize that whatever Jesus suffered in the flesh, he endured all for me. I am likewise aware that I am consoled and have greatly benefitted from all the good that the Virgin had done in her life, all the holy services she had rendered unto Christ, and all the trials she and Jesus had endured together in this world.

Chosen Mother, hold on your lap your beloved and only Son, who suffered a cruel death for me, and keep him there for a time, before he is placed in the tomb, while I, on bended knee, adore him here on earth. I pour out my prayers before him and kiss his wounds and limbs, disfigured by martyrdom. Hear me, my Lady; be merciful to me, answer my prayers, and offer your Son to me that I may kiss him, who so loved my soul.

Chapter 34

Prayers to members of Christ's body

His feet

O admirable feet of my Lord Jesus Christ, transfixed by having one hard nail driven into both of them, and from which there flowed a copious amount of your precious blood, I reverently adore you and heartily kiss you, asking you to pardon whatever I have committed while standing or walking.

Hail Mary . . .

His legs

O graceful legs and humble knees of my Lord Jesus Christ, so often bent in prayer or prostrate on the naked earth, and struck by stiff switches during your Passion, I humbly adore you and meekly kiss you, asking you to forgive my sins of lukewarmness and laziness in serving you.

Hail Mary . . .

His torso

O holy and pure torso of my Lord Jesus Christ, that the virginal womb of Holy Mary carried and nursed, and so bitterly beaten by many a lash, I rightly adore you

HISTORSO and compassionately kiss you, asking you to free me from my sins of having shown more care for my body than necessary.

Hail Mary . . .

His side

O honored side of my Lord Jesus Christ, wherein the deeply pierced wound of divine love stands open, I especially adore you and devoutly kiss you, pleading that you pardon my sins against fraternal charity and of growing cold in my love for heavenly things.

Hail Mary . . .

His back

O most patient back of my Lord Jesus Christ, ever ready to carry, and without complaint, the wood of life and the burden of all our sins, and enduring the brutal blows of the scourges, I lovingly adore you and with sadness in my heart I pray that you remit my sins of being impatient in bearing my everyday burdens.

Hail Mary . . .

His hands

O venerable hands of my Lord Jesus Christ, that for a long time were stretched out on the Cross and pierced by large iron nails, I faithfully adore you and with tears in my eyes I kiss you as I request you to absolve me of my sins committed by action or touch.

Hail Mary . . .

His breast

O most pure breast of my Lord Jesus Christ, in which there was no stain of sin and into which none could enter, and upon which Blessed John the Apostle leaned during the Last Supper, I sincerely adore you and affectionately kiss you, beseeching you to cleanse me of my sins committed by fostering foul thoughts.

Hail Mary . . .

His neck

O white and delicate neck of my Lord Jesus Christ, frequently lean because of hunger and thirst, never ornately adorned nor held proudly upright, but always held in humble and reverent subjection to father and mother, and harshly buffeted in your Passion, I humbly adore you and lovingly kiss you as I pray that you forgive my sins committed out of vain motives.

Hail Mary . . .

His mouth

O gentle mouth of my Lord Jesus Christ, from whom the word of salvation came to our world, and besmirched by the spittle of the populace and embittered by the cup of vinegar, I adore you and kindly ask you to forgive my sins committed in eating, drinking, and speaking.

Hail Mary . . .

His face

O handsome face of my Lord Jesus Christ, full of benevolent friendliness, shamefully spat upon by the crowds, brutally slapped and shockingly veiled, I lovingly adore you and affectionately kiss you, asking you to pardon my sins of disrespect and irreverence committed against you.

Hail Mary . . .

His ears

O fortunate ears of my Lord Jesus Christ, never yielding to flattery nor permitting any unbecoming or harmful word to turn you away from the path of righteousness, I honorably adore you and fervently kiss you asking you to forgive my sins of yielding to flattering speech and improper language.

Hail Mary . . .

His eyes

O brightly shining eyes of my Lord Jesus Christ, innocent of all unseemly desires and now sealed by violent death, and whence frequently came a shower of tears, I heartily adore you and gently kiss you beseeching you to forgive all my sins committed by the immodest use of my eyes.

Hail Mary . . .

His head

O sublime and revered head of my Lord Jesus Christ, wearing a crown of sharp thorns pressed deeply into it, with hair stained and consecrated by the blood that had flowed therefrom, together with the angels and all the powers of heaven I adore you and ardently kiss each of your sacred wounds, and from the depths of my heart I ask you to free me from all the thorns of sin that remain in me and that you deign to number me, though I am the least, among your elect.

Hail Mary . . .

Chapter 35

On the reverent burial
of the Lord Jesus

LORD JESUS CHRIST, Essence of life and the Radiance of everlasting life, I bless and thank you for the attentive anointing of your body with precious aromatic spices. Though this was not necessary to stave off your body's corruption, it was, nevertheless, most acceptable to you because your faithful friends did it out of love and because it was done in accordance with Jewish custom, for we read that there were patriarchs and kings who were so anointed before burial.

I praise and glorify you for the meticulous wrapping of your sacred body in a spotless shroud as well as for the careful covering of your sacred head with a pure white napkin, later found in the holy sepulcher.

I praise and glorify you for your being carried amid tears to the place of burial, for your being reverently lowered and humbly positioned in a new tomb that was hewn out of a rock and given you by Joseph, the distinguished senator. Since the hour was then growing late, you were honorably buried there with much wailing and securely closed within by a huge stone.

Venerable Joseph, rejoice because the task you accomplished was most holy and gave you the opportunity to express your unspeakable love for Christ. Indeed, I am most grateful to you and I laudably commend your noble character in doing what you have done and for carrying it out in a most dignified and deferential manner. Not only did you request Pilate's permission to bury Jesus' body, but you also offered your own sepulcher, which you had prepared for yourself and in which you expected to be placed after your own death.

How greatly God must have cherished you, for him, whose power extends over the entire world and over all that is contained in the heavenly orbits, to choose to be buried in your tomb, rather than in any other place on earth. Most illustrious of men, I tell you that as long as this world lasts and there are faithful on the earth, you will be held in honor before God and men.

This sacred sepulcher will become more glorious and celebrated than those of saints and kings and will be spoken of as being the most acclaimed in all the world. From all the corners of the earth countless pilgrims will come to this holy place to worship at the very spot where the Lord's body once rested. Here Jesus was placed and here the Crucified was buried. Here the women mourned him and here the soldiers were set to guard him. Here Christ rose on the third day and Mary Magdalen saw him and here the heavenly angel of the Lord appeared. And here, those guarding the tomb were terrified and became as dead men.

And you, my soul, remain here at the tomb for a little while and join the women in mourning the Lord Jesus, who was buried for you. It is only fitting that you lament him, from whom you desire to receive the reward of eternal joy.

Consider how dolefully all of Christ's friends grieved for him, especially the holy women, and particularly when he was taken from them and when they saw him sealed in the sepulcher. It was because of their love for him that they had set all things aside and followed him far and wide throughout that land, and it was to him that they so generously ministered from their own means. It was because they were so devoted to him that they could not endure being separated from his comforting presence, not even for a short time. It was with him that they desired to spend their lives and engage in holy conversation, and it was because of him that they believed that they could be forever blessed. The more intense the love, the more bitter the grief!

The affliction that these women suffered more than any other was that their hope of having Jesus rise again now seemed taken from them. Their faith was, somehow, buried along with Jesus in the tomb. The only consolation left to these poor dejected women was, so they thought, to mourn the dead Jesus or to begin preparing the spices for his body. If they were unable to bring him back to life again, at least they might, by assiduous anointing, keep his body from corrupting.

O you holy and pious women, whose love for Christ is without end, do not lament excessively and do not yield to despair. Recall Jesus' words, which he himself spoke, and wait a bit longer, for after three days he will undoubtedly rise. You, who now lament him who was buried in pain and sadness, will see him in all his brilliance, and your hearts will again overflow with happiness. His friends, now extremely saddened over his death and burial, will experience a newfound joy. Jesus will no longer have any need of your anointing because risen from the dead he will appear in absolute glory; he will be clothed in the robe of immortality and death will no longer have any power over him.

And you, learn from Jesus' burial to think profitably about your own body's demise. It is necessary to commit to earth, whatever is received from it; *You are dust and unto dust you will return.*[1] What do you have to be proud about, when you will soon be the object of decay and will have to be covered with earth? What are you looking for in this world, you who are soon to be cast out of it and trodden underfoot by men?

When you come upon the graves of the dead, remember that you will soon be joining them. That is the designated home for all the living. There the rich man and the poor man will be stretched out on a common bed and both will be content with only a small patch of earth. No distinction will be made there between the nobleman and the commoner, and the weak will no longer be stomped upon by the more powerful. There the miser will no longer benefit from his money, nor will the clever profit from his cunning. There the prim will become the food of worms, and the dandy will give off an offensive odor. And those who have placed themselves on pedestals will be brought low and the praise that the proud were accustomed to will no longer be theirs. Take notice how all mortals tend toward nothing and how all flesh, made corrupt by sin, returns to its original source.

Therefore, strive so to live and through the spirit to mortify your flesh, that when your body turns into dust your soul will be judged worthy to rest in blessed peace. If you live your life in labor and sorrow on a Good Friday, you will have a restful Holy Saturday and then a most joyful Easter Sunday, the day of the resurrection of the just.

The more austerely you live in the world, so much more tranquil will be your repose in the grave. The more firmly you cling to the Cross, so much more assurance you have of reaching Christ. The more bitterly you deplore your sins, so much less will remain to be purged by the avenging flames. So lament during this time of grace, when the doors of mercy are open, and when God, in whom there is abundant

[1] Genesis 3:19.

redemption, accepts your repentance. Mourn also the wretched condition of the world and the incredible indifference of men. Only a few are found today to be true followers of the Crucified, and many permit their original spiritual fervor to grow cold.

Let meditating on Jesus Christ and him crucified be your daily prayer. Keep Jesus always before your eyes and keep ever near the foot of his Cross. Whether in life or in death, enter the tomb with Jesus so that when Christ, who is your life, shall appear again, you will rise with him in glory. Amen.

ART CREDITS